STILL REIGNING

STILL REIGNING

THOUGHTS OF A QUEEN

THE QUEEN

[of twitter @queen_uk]

Overlook Duckworth
New York • London

First published in the US and the UK in 2014 by
Overlook Duckworth

NEW YORK
141 Wooster Street
New York, NY 10012
www.overlookpress.com
For bulk and special sales please contact
sales@overlookny.com,
or write us at the above address.

LONDON
30 Calvin Street, London E1 6NW
T: 020 7490 7300
E: info@duckworth-publishers.co.uk
www.ducknet.co.uk
For bulk and special sales please contact
sales@duckworth-publishers.co.uk,
or write to us at the above address.

Cataloguing-in-Publication Data is available
from the Library of Congress

A catalogue record for this book is available
from the British Library

ISBNs
US: 978-1-4683-0940-9
UK: 978-0-7156-4913-8

Typeset by Ray Davies
Manufactured in the United States of America

For those about to rock,
one salutes you.

Contents

Contents

2. Politics

3. Celebrity

Contents

4. Royal Travel and Foreign Affairs

5. Events, Occasions and Other Things

Contents

6. Letters from Her Majesty

7. From the Royal Notebook

Contents

Foreword

Still Reigning

Queen of sixteen sovereign nations, Head of the Commonwealth of 54 independent states, Supreme Governor of the Church of England, Defender of the Faith, wife to the DoE, mother, grandmother, great-grandmother. Yes, one is kept rather busy.

One was up a tree in Kenya when one ascended the Throne. It's often said that one went up a Princess and came down a Queen and since then it's been all go. Reigning nine to five, what a way to make a living.

Of course, most of one's time is taken up by the United Kingdom, Canada, New Zealand and

Australia. One's Caribbean territories seem to cope quite well without any discernable sign of a Government and one only has to check in occasionally to make sure they haven't been taken by the French.

But it hasn't all been plain sailing, one doesn't mind telling you. One's father, King George VI, always used to say, "Lillibet, when you become Queen, always remember: politicians are mental." Oh, how right he was. There have been a few over the years that one quite liked (well, one actually: Winston Churchill), but it's mainly been a bit of a struggle.

Elected representatives are a bit like teenagers: all of a sudden they're all grown up and know the answer to everything and think they're invincible and one can't tell them anything without them bursting into tears, screaming "It's so unfair, you don't know anything," and running out of the room.

It's not easy having a Cabinet of school children here in the UK. If it's not Tom and Jerry (Mr Cameron and Mr Clegg) falling out with one another it's Count Duckula (Mr Osborne) sodding up a budget. Still, his counting skills are coming on wonderfully (he can get to ten now if he uses both hands and both feet).

One has to cope with the odd bit of drama at Downing Street, like when Mr Clegg dropped his Etch-a-Sketch into the paddling pool, thus practically bringing the Liberal Democrats to a complete standstill. He hadn't been that upset since his knob fell off (of his Etch-a-Sketch). Not that Mr Bean (Ed Miliband) is much better. Poor chap has never really recovered from his trip to Afghanistan when the troops all thought he was a stand-up comedian doing an impression of his brother. Awkward.

Of course, one's elected representatives aren't the only things one has had to contend with. Shortly after one ascended the Throne, it became apparent that empire was becoming something of an unfashionable national pastime. And so began many years of "pretending not to be in charge".

It's stressful, one can assure you. No sooner are representatives of the people across the world elected than one has to gently break the news to them that the British Empire is alive and well; that we've just been "playing it down" a little. There's disappointment, understandably, but usually followed by relief.

President Obama was overjoyed, actually. Got straight on the phone the second he was elected and practically begged one to take the reins. Poor chap talked without taking a breath for about fifteen minutes before one could get a word in edgeways and reassure him that democracy, much like *Coronation Street*, was a fictional concept designed to entertain the masses, and that the British Monarch was still very much in the driving seat.

And the media. The sodding media. One doesn't know what's worse: the relentless press intrusion or the generation of "celebrities" they've created. There was a time when concerts at the Palace were organised by world-renowned composers. These days we get Gary Barlow (who, incidentally, spends more time drinking tea than he does on the job. He's like a bloody builder. "Oooo that's going to cost more than we'd estimated, yer maj." And he owes a palace load of tax).

And then there's the family. The Royal Family. The Firm. A beacon of righteousness and decorum in our society. When they're not naked in Las Vegas, sunbathing topless in France, or abseiling down buildings, that is.

We've got a new member of the family now though. Someone who has come into our lives as a result of William and Catherine's love: Mrs "Queen-Mother-in-Waiting" Middleton. Oh, and there's Prince George. We've already started preparing the little chap for "Kingdom". As the DoE says to Prince William, "He may be all shit and nappies now, but that boy will be Emperor of India one day."

Yes, it is a funny old world, being a Queen. But despite it all, one's still here. Still in charge; still iconic; still on the gin; still ruling the world. Still reigning.

God Save One.

1

The Royal Family

Prince Philip,
Duke of Edinburgh
(The DoE)

His Royal Highness The Prince Philip,
Duke of Edinburgh, Duke of Hazard, Earl
of Merioneth, Baron Greenwich, Baron
Greenback, Royal Knight of the Most Noble
Order of the Garter, Auric Goldfinger,
Extra Knight of the Most Ancient and Most
Noble Order of the Thistle, Protector of
the Daffodil, Grand Master and First and
Principal Knight Grand Cross of the Most
Excellent Order of the British Empire, Pussy
Galore, Member of the Order of Merit, Knight
Rider, Companion of the Order of Australia,
Additional Member of the Order of New
Zealand, Extra Companion of the Queen's
Service Order, Royal Chief of the Order of

Logohu, Extraordinary Companion of the Order of Canada, Colonel Hannibal Smith, Extraordinary Commander of the Order of Military Merit, Canadian Forces Decoration, Lord of Her Majesty's Most Honourable Privy Council, Privy Councillor of the Queen's Privy Council for Canada, Personal Aide-de-Camp to Her Majesty, Lord High Admiral of the United Kingdom.

Or, as one calls him, the DoE.

It was 1939 that one met the DoE. Of course, he wasn't the DoE then, but he was a Prince (of Greece, admittedly, but nobody's perfect). One's father, King George VI, and one's mother, Queen Elizabeth, had popped down to the Royal Naval College at Dartmouth to pick up a consignment of Champagne that the Navy had picked up (acquired/pillaged) from France. During the visit, they asked Philip to keep an eye on oneself and Margaret. Well, to cut a long story short, he fell in love with one's majesty, amongst other things, and one felt it would be wrong to leave him in Greece.

Eventually, in the summer of 1946, Philip asked the King for one's hand in marriage and the King said he could have all of one as he'd asked so nicely. We did have to strip him of his Greek and Danish royal titles though, mainly for reasons of a "they-sounded-ridiculous" nature, and have him adopt the surname Mountbatten so he sounded a bit more British.

One's engagement was announced to the public on 10 July 1947. On the day before one's Wedding, the King bestowed the style His Royal Highness on Philip and on the morning of the wedding, 20 November 1947, he was made Duke of Edinburgh, Duke of Hazard, Earl of Merioneth, and Baron Greenback of Dangermouse in the County of London.

Nearly seventy years later, one is still with the old chap. Yes, in this time there is not a swear word he has not uttered, a nation he has not offended, a politician he has not berated or an animal he has not shot. But he has been by one's side through thick and thin, his charities have provided support and comfort and encouragement and opportunity to many millions of people and his forthright and unbridled humour has endeared him to one's millions of subjects around the world.

One has become so used to being accompanied by the DoE, walking two steps behind, and it wasn't really until one had to go it alone that one realised how much one relies on the old fellow.

In 2013 one officially opened New Broadcasting House for the BBC, delivered Bruce Forsyth's redundancy notice, explained to BBC News that Justin sodding Bieber arriving late for a concert is not national breaking news and dropped off Prince Harry's audition tape for *Strictly Come Dancing*, though the poor DoE has such an aversion to journalists that he opted for a two-week stay in hospital instead. Although he said he was tempted to come along and find out if there are any celebrities from the 1970s who have avoided arrest and are still working there.

Couldn't help but be a little worried though, one doesn't mind telling you. One was watching him at the Buckingham Palace garden party the week before, operating the BBQ/flamethrower as usual whilst Prince Edward laid out the fairy cakes, and wondering what on earth one would do without him.

Although to be quite honest, it's probably best if someone else does the garden party BBQs in future. He likes to soak the coal in petrol ("to get it going") and in 1982 managed to set fire to the Archbishop of Canterbury. Luckily we were able to pop him in the lake to put out the flames and he was very understanding about the whole thing – baptism of fire and all that.

That said, there is not a prince on the planet who can BBQ a burger like the DoE. Although even he was unable to do anything with the box of value frozen sausages that Mr and Mrs Middleton brought up to Balmoral in 2011. They'd had them in the caravan freezer for ages, apparently, and thought they'd better use them up. Thankfully Philip managed to swap them for a box of Fortnum and Mason's whilst no one was looking and slung the lot over a hedge. Camilla was devastated, she said she would have taken them back for credit and stocked up on gin if she had known.

Yes, it is at times like this that one appreciates those around one. The DoE has, through these many years, been one's liegeman and greatest comfort, inspiration and support. One's DoE. We owe him a great debt of gratitude.

Prince Charles, Prince of Wales

His Royal Highness The Prince Charles Philip Arthur George, Prince of Wales and Earl of Chester, Duke of Cornwall, Duke of Rothesay, Earl of Carrick, Baron of Renfrew, Lord of the Isles, Prince and Great Steward of Scotland, Royal Knight Companion of the Most Noble Order of the Garter, Royal Knight Companion of the Most Ancient and Most Noble Order of the Thistle, Knight Grand Cross of the Most Honourable Order of the Bath, Member of the Order of Merit, Knight of the Order of Australia, Companion of the Queen's Service Order, Member of Her Majesty's Most Honourable Privy Council, Aide-de-Camp to Her Majesty.

We don't say that all the time though. He's generally just "Charles", although the DoE does like to use the full title when telling him off, seems to have a bit more impact somehow.

He's always been something of a pain in the arse if one's being honest. When he was small he used to have this awful habit of knighting inanimate objects. There were more Knights of the Action Men than there were Knights of the Garter at one point. We had to put our foot down when he became a teenager and developed a close attachment to plants though. One simply cannot have ennobled vegetables, not in a civilized society. That kind of thing might be perfectly acceptable on the continent but over here on the right side of the Channel a sprout is a sprout and a politician is a cabbage and that's that.

The DoE was a bit worried about him until the age of about fifteen. Thought he needed a bit of toughening up, "a bit too weedy to stand up to the Germans" and suchlike. We needn't have worried. He came back from boarding school at eighteen positively filled with testosterone. Honestly, we thought we had another Henry VIII on our hands for a while there.

It was like an Engelbert Humperdinck concert at Buckingham Palace some nights; women throwing their knickers at him and all sorts. Poor old Andrew, who was at an impressionable age at the time (and ever since, come to think of it) tried his best to get in on the act but only really managed to catch the odd passing bra.

To be fair to Charles, he's turned out a good lad, especially after the Diana business. One was very fond of Diana and one can't help but wonder what would have happened if she'd given up the teddy bear when they were married, as Charles had wanted. There were three of them in that marriage, you see, and it was a bit crowded. No man wants to share his bed with a princess and a five-foot Winnie-the-Pooh bear. Well, Nick Clegg does, but that's another matter.

And if there is one thing The Prince of Wales is undeniably good at, it's baking. All those years glued to the TV whilst *Blue Peter* was on had an enormous influence (and one is not just talking about the crown made from an old washing up bottle and two loo rolls that he wears at dinner to this very day – the DoE says it's the closest he'll be getting to a real crown anytime soon). He was barely out of short trousers when he baked his first Duchy Original biscuit.

How he finds the time, one will never know. Not only does he farm the ingredients himself (all by hand – he absolutely refuses to buy a combine harvester – Camilla steers the plough whilst Charles rides the horse. She swears it does wonders for upper body strength), but he spends hours in the Highgrove kitchen baking those little biscuits and filling up jars of jam. He's like the Mary Berry of Royalty, only with a significantly soggier bottom on occasion.

Not sure if William will carry on the tradition when he becomes Prince of Wales though, although Mr Middleton has apparently trademarked the name "Middleton Originals" just in case there's an opportunity to develop the online party supplies business to food. He said he didn't want to push the boat out and buy a new van until it was established, but felt confident he could fit an air-conditioning unit to the roof if required under food hygiene laws. So that's a relief.

Since Charles has settled with Camilla, we've finally got round to the business of preparing him for Kingship. One's been bringing him to work on Tuesdays so he can start to get the hang of reigning. We've started him off on administrative tasks, like Papua New Guinea for example, where he can't do too much damage. Although one's got to watch him all the time. One popped out for a toasted cheese and tomato sandwich one lunchtime and came back to find he'd pressed the wrong button and almost partitioned France. As if President Chirac wasn't nervous enough at the time, poor chap.

Say what you like about Prince Charles, he does like to keep busy. If he's not out in the garden weeding something, he's writing letters to ministers. Fortunately, they can't read his handwriting so no damage is ever done, but it does succeed in wasting a bit of Government time, at least. One always thinks that whilst the Government is answering Prince Charles' letters, they're not thinking up new ways to piss off the electorate and that alone is a worthy use of a Prince of Wales.

Camilla, Duchess of Cornwall

Her Royal Highness The Duchess of Cornwall, Duchess of Rothmans, Duchess of Gin, Countess of Chester, Dame Grand Cross of the Royal Victorian Order.

Camilla is what we in the Royal Family like to call "a bloody good laugh". Since marrying The Prince of Wales in 2005, she has taken over from Her Late Majesty Queen Elizabeth the Queen Mother as Director of Fun.

The highlight of the Royal party calendar is Camilla's annual "tarts and vicars" party at Clarence House, which happens each year on the early May Bank Holiday. The occasion is marked by plumes of cigar smoke rising from the Clarence House chimney (which caused a bit of confusion with Cardinal Nichols, the

Archbishop of Westminster, last year when he thought we were electing a new Pope).

Princesses Beatrice and Eugenie were first to arrive, complete with the usual comedy hats. They like to turn up early and get a seat and usually bring a magnum of vodka, which is always welcome. Unfortunately, Princes William and Harry couldn't join us last year due to being on an unofficial (and in the case of Prince Harry, "unclothed") visit to the United States for a stag weekend. William got the wrong end of the stick and thought it was actually a stag-hunting weekend and so took his gun with him, which caused a few problems at Heathrow.

Ironically for a tarts and vicars party, the Archbishop of Canterbury arrived dressed as a vicar, which struck one as deeply unimaginative. Thankfully Andrew took up the tart cause and arrived looking like an extra from the Rocky Horror Show.

The DoE is in charge of the food, which usually consists of barbecuing "the arse end of a bloody great big cow" over a fire so large it makes the Windsor Castle blaze look like a campfire. No idea how he gets the flames so large. Camilla thinks it's probably the petrol.

Bit of an awkward moment when the Archbishop's vestments caught fire whilst he was roasting a marshmallow. Luckily he managed to plunge himself into the Clarence House fishpond before too much damage was done. The DoE found it all wonderfully amusing though and said that burning priests was a "bloody good British tradition" that we ought to seriously consider bringing back. Mentioned it to the Pope but he didn't seem keen.

After supper, we all sit around the epic fire for a few verses of "Ging gang goolie goolie goolie goolie watcha, Ging gang goo, ging gang goo. Ging gang goolie goolie goolie goolie watcha, Ging gang goo, ging gang goo. Hayla, hayla shayla, hayla shayla, shayla, oh-ho. Hayla, hayla shayla, hayla shayla, shayla, oh". Mr Cameron finds the whole thing very stressful as he finds it almost impossible to remember the words.

The whole thing usually goes on until about 4am, although Andrew had to head to bed early. Something about needing to Knight the Bishop or raising the standard or something.

Not sure what happened to Camilla. She was last seen trying to launch fireworks into the Treasury building from a tree house in the Clarence House garden. Apparently she was found about three days later in a front garden in Staines, along with seven horses, an entire massed military band and a cigar bigger than a marrow.

Prince Edward, Earl of Wessex

His Royal Highness The Prince Edward Antony Richard Louise, Earl of Wessex, Viscount Mint Biscuit, Royal Knight Companion of the Most Noble Order of the Garter, Willy Wonka, Knight Grand Cross of the Royal Victorian Order, Aide-de-Very-Camp to Her Majesty.

In 1963, we decided that an heir and a spare wasn't enough and so belt and braces and all that, the DoE decided to order a third son. Prince Edward arrived in 1964.

It was in about 1975 that we discovered Edward's talent for acting. The annual Royal Household pantomime, renowned in chattering circles as almost as enjoyable as a general election, was taking place at Buckingham Palace as usual and Edward was making his debut.

Royal Household pantomimes have been a tradition since the time of Queen Elizabeth I, who came up with the idea at the trial of Mary Queen of Scots whilst listening to opposing sides shouting "Oh no she didn't; oh yes she did" when exploring if she had been guilty of a plot to murder the Queen, and later when during the execution the crowd saw the swordsman and shouted "He's behind you!"

In 1975, we were planning a full-scale enactment of the Battle of Agincourt but Edward suggested at the last minute that we scrap that and produce our own 480-minute opera based on Queen's 'Bohemian Rhapsody', which had just been released. After a quick meeting of the Privy Council to sanction the decision, the young Edward got working on a script and musical score and within six weeks we were ready to rock.

To this day, one still remembers the look on Freddie Mercury's face when, after about seven hours, a sequined Edward descended from a chandelier in the ballroom singing "I see a little silhouetto of a man...". Freddie Mercury was to adopt a similar moustache himself of course in later years, a trend that Edward has always been very proud of starting.

After a quick and ultimately rather awkward spell in the armed forces, Edward took up employment with Andrew Lloyd Webber. Sadly it didn't last.

In 1993, Edward met Sophie Rhys-Jones, a Public Relations agent, at a charity event. They bonded over a love of the Carpenters and began their relationship on a rainy day and Monday soon afterwards. Their engagement was announced on 6 January 1999. Edward proposed to Sophie with an engagement ring forged from the finest copper. The wedding took place on 19 June of the same year at St George's Chapel at Windsor Castle.

One is never sure what to buy as a wedding gift, but in the end decided on *The Complete A-Team* on DVD box set and creating Edward Earl of Wessex and Viscount Severn (Viscounts one to six were taken).

Since marriage, Edward's love of theatre has continued to thrive. He particularly enjoyed the 2013 primetime TV edition of the Punch and Judy Show; otherwise known as the Nigel Farage and Nick Clegg Europe Debate for BBC2, and the 2014 tragedy, when Mr Clegg lost all but one of his MEPs in the European Elections.

Prince Andrew, Duke of York

His Royal Highness The Prince Andrew Albert Christian Edward, Grand Old Duke of York, Earl of Inverness, Baron Killyleagh, Knight Companion of the Most Noble Order of the Garter, Beverley Sister, Commander of Ten Thousand Men, Knight Grand Cross of the Royal Victorian Order, Canadian Forces Decoration, Spare Heir, Aide-de-Camp to Her Majesty.

It's often unfairly said that Prince Andrew is a "Playboy Prince". This is entirely untrue. In fact, he has never been in *Playboy*, although one suspects he has bought a copy on the odd occasion.

Andrew, in fact, is something of a hero, having been a helicopter pilot with the Royal Navy in the Falklands War. Mrs Thatcher wasn't actually at all bothered about the Falklands at the time but if there's one thing Prince Andrew cannot abide it's an Argentine invasion. He took matters into his own hands, fired up the chopper and was bombing them before anyone realised what had happened.

The original purpose of the task force sent to the South Atlantic was to get him back before anyone managed to shoot him down, which would have been awkward to say the least. However, once there we decided we might as well finish the job and liberate the Falklands before coming home. Mrs Thatcher took all the credit, of course. Not that Andrew minded. He flew himself back to Britain, firing a few warning shots at the French on route.

It was Christmas 1985 when Andrew won Sarah Ferguson in a cracker. After trying unsuccessfully to swap her for a pack of miniature playing cards, he decided to keep her and they were married in March 1986.

Can't help but think the Duchess of York got a rather hard time from the press. It was the 1980s and anti-ginger feeling was at an all time high. Whilst the eyes of the world were on apartheid in South Africa, it was almost impossible for a ginger person to get a seat on the bus in London.

That said, it all went rather well until about 1992 when Sarah made the enormous error of booking a rather expensive pedicure, during which the feet are cleaned and exfoliated by a specially trained tongue. Sadly *The Sun* got hold of a photo and assumed it were something sexual. We all agreed that the truth was simply too bizarre to reveal and so a divorce was decided to be the least embarrassing way out.

They have remained firm friends ever since though and have provided one with two absolutely delightful (hat fashion aside) princesses. Say what you like about Prince Andrew, but he cannot be faulted for his dedication as a father.

He is, however, rather unpredictable. One was enjoying an award-winning lie-in one morning, (thanks to a Highland Games/gin induced hangover), when Prince Andrew called from an official visit to the Shard in London where he'd found himself on the 87th floor when the lift broke down.

What is it about Dukes of York and high places? The DoE says we haven't had this much trouble since a previous Grand Old Duke of York marched 10,000 men up to the top of the hill, but at least he managed to march them down again.

After much deliberation, it was decided that the only way forward would be for Andrew to abseil down the 1,000ft drop. Prince Harry (who at the time had been literally and metaphorically grounded since his Las Vegas trip) suggested Andrew try it in the nude but we quickly discounted that as a suggestion.

Prince Andrew, Duke of York

Andrew is actually something of an abseiling
pro, having mastered escaping from the Duchess
of York by tying bed sheets together and sliding
down the walls of Windsor Castle, so once
he got over the edge he was apparently quite
comfortable. He stopped half way down for a
bacon sandwich that someone passed through
an open window and said the view was lovely.
The DoE said he's always had his head in the
clouds.

Prince William and Catherine, Duke and Duchess of Cambridge

His Royal Highness The Prince William Arthur Philip Louis, Duke of Cambridge, Earl of Strathearn, Baron Carrickfergus, Inspector Gadget, Royal Knight Companion of the Most Noble Order of the Garter, Knight of the Roundtable, Knight of the Most Ancient and Most Noble Order of the Thistle, Personal Aide-de-Camp to Her Majesty the Queen, and Her Royal Highness The Duchess of Cambridge, Countess of Strathearn, Acting Deputy Assistant Head Retailer at Middleton Online Party Things Ltd and Lady Carrickfergus.

Prince William, of course, is second in line to one's throne, after his father Prince Charles. He's very much like his mother, the late Princess of Wales. In fact the DoE says he was lucky to inherit his mother's looks, humour, compassion and manner and his father's claim to the throne; best of both worlds.

There is great pressure on heirs to the throne, of course. Thankfully when one were a little Princess one's uncle was destined for the throne and so one managed a fairly normal upbringing before the abdication crisis put one's father in charge and thrust one up the line of succession, so to speak. William though has had to cope with the expectation from day one. All in all, he's done a bloody good job.

The education for Kingship is a closely guarded secret, but it basically involves letting them reign as regent in countries where they generally can only do a limited amount of damage to get the hang of it. William was, in fact, reigning regent in Barbados between the ages of four and seven, although we kept it close to our chests. And the rum did wonders in getting him to sleep through the night.

Of course, he really came into his own when he went to St Andrew's University in Scotland to study for his degree. It was there that he found Catherine Middleton. Or, more accurately, she found him.

Mrs "I'm going to be Queen Mother if it sodding well kills me" Middleton had fired her off like a heat-seeking missile to secure him, apparently. Poor chap was helpless. One minute he's sitting there with a nice gin and tonic watching a fashion show and the next he's presented with Catherine Middleton in a see-through dress coming at him like a rocket sled on rails. Still, all's well that ends well.

Despite a somewhat on/off relationship at first, William and Catherine have made a lovely couple. One remembers hearing tales of weekends away with the Middletons in their caravan during the summer holidays. Mr Middleton would hook it up to his transit van, let William choose a destination and off they'd go. One still has a collection of postcards from their trips to Brighton, Blackpool, Skegness, Scarborough, Bournemouth and other areas where there's a worryingly high number of Liberal Democrat and Green Party voters etc.

Apparently, a highlight of the trips was Mr Middleton setting up his portable miniature golf course outside the caravan whilst Pippa knocked up a tasty treat of blackened sausages and curried baked beans on a gas stove.

It was actually during one of these trips that Prince Harry joined them and discovered the Brighton nude beach. No sooner had they arrived than he had the orb and sceptre out glistening in the sun.

Still, duty calls and after St Andrew's William went off to Sandhurst to complete his training as an officer and a pilot, before helicopter flying training to become a full-time pilot with the Search and Rescue Force.

For many years, William and Catherine were able to live like an ordinary couple, with a little 400-acre estate and a small staff of only 700 people on Anglesey, where he worked as a Search and Rescue pilot. The irony wasn't lost on one: William in a helicopter in Wales saving people and Harry in Afghanistan in a helicopter shooting at them. That's the key to Royalty: cover all bases.

Finally, William married Catherine on 29 April 2011 at Westminster Abbey. One wasn't sure what to buy that would be of any use so in the end decided to make him Duke of Cambridge, Earl of Strathearn, Inspector Gadget and Baron Carrickfergus. (Baron Carrickfergus is actually his favourite title; thinks it makes him sound like a Bond villain. We only let him use it on the continent though; it does keep the Spanish on their toes.)

Their wedding day started off a bit chaotic, to be honest. King Simeon II of Bulgaria insisted on cooking everyone breakfast, which was kind, and the Crown Prince of the Netherlands emerged wearing what one can only describe politely as an "alternative" outfit. Sent him upstairs to change immediately – we can't have that kind of thing in Westminster Abbey and that is the end of it. The Duchess of Kent wouldn't know where to look, though Camilla did offer to tell her.

All went well at the Abbey, although come to think of it there was something of a major seating plan error. Whilst Mr Cameron and Mr Clegg were virtually hidden from the entire congregation and unable to see anything of the service, they were in one's direct line of sight. Not sure how one managed to miss that. It is a bit distracting, spending an entire service with Mr Clegg waving like a man possessed as if he's trying to form another coalition or something.

One doesn't remember much about the service itself, mainly because one spent most of it feeling slightly awkward about Princess Beatrice's giant hat, which mildly resembled some kind of ancient Egyptian crown/children's party snack.

Of course, now they have a family, the Carrickferguses can't possibly be expected to live in such a little house on Anglesey, so one's given them Princess Diana's former apartment in Kensington Palace. Gave it a quick £25million lick of paint first; can't have them having flashbacks to the Middletons' caravan.

Prince George

Like every good Royal, the new-kid-on-the-succession-block was bringing joy to millions before he was even born. We announced the upcoming birth on the first Monday in December 2012. Seeing as half the country was either under water or freezing bloody cold, one agreed to cheer everyone up a bit by giving the green light on announcing that the Duke and Duchess of Cambridge were expecting an heir.

The DoE and I knew for a while, of course. William was thrilled when Catherine broke the news, although he did originally think she'd said, "You're going to have new hair", which he was equally excited about. Alas no miracle hair replacement treatment (probably just as well, Elton John has never been the same since having his done) but the joyous news that we had a Royal baby to look forward to.

Charles was simply ecstatic, of course. He texted Harry (who was serving with the British Army/ sunbathing in Afghanistan at the time) to let him know the news before telling the media. He replied to say he was over the moon and was going to take his chopper out to show the locals in celebration.

Mrs "we're all family now, I do hope you'll call me Carole" Middleton called to say that she and Mr Middleton were delighted that their genes would be contributing to a future monarch. As luck would have it, they were doing a discount on christening party balloons and napkins at their online shop and she'd put some aside in case one wanted to order at a later date (prices excluded postage and packaging, apparently). We never did.

The Prime Minister, Mr Cameron, was also thrilled. He texted to say that the news had come at a wonderful time and that he hoped it might divert some headlines away from the economy, borrowing figures, press regulation report etc., all of which were causing the poor chap some discomfort at the time. Nice to see he had his priorities straight.

Even the Pope got in on the action by announcing he was joining Twitter. As Supreme Governor of the Church of England, one has been tweeting for years, of course, but it usually takes the Catholics a while to catch up and get with the programme on these things.

He said it was in celebration of the coming Royal birth, but the DoE thinks he just wanted some of the limelight for himself. Not sure he took to social media well, incidentally: within three months he'd become the first Pope ever to abdicate. One did tell him he could have just deactivated the Twitter account, but he must have been confused.

After a quick scan to check the heir was a boy, we announced that the baby would become monarch even if a girl.

That said, there is little doubt that Queens make better monarchs. As Elizabeth I famously said, "I may have the weak and feeble body of a woman but I can drink you bastards under the table."

However, it was generally considered that the Church of England, who despite having a woman as Supreme Governor struggle with the whole women in authority thing, would have found the whole thing a little much to handle if it were a girl so we were relieved there was a little prince on the way.

Six months into the Royal pregnancy and the Duchess of Cambridge was blossoming. Prince William says she had a perfect bump, which ironically was almost exactly the same size as Prince Andrew's belly (although he was not, as far as we were aware, expecting anything significant – a job, a baby, a wife etc.).

Mrs "I'm about to become grandmother to a future monarch, I do wish you'd call me Carole" Middleton was beside herself with excitement. She'd spent a small fortune in Toys R Us, so much so that Mr Middleton had to get a bigger van to transport it all. Honestly, the shed at Kensington Palace looked like the set of *Toy Story*.

Prince Edward didn't help matters. He donated his entire My Little Pony collection, complete with My First Stable house. Poor Catherine looked like the world had ended when he took it out of the boot of the Range Rover but she managed to say thank you and that she was sure the heir would enjoy playing with them.

Of course, all this happened at a time when we had a new Archbishop of Canterbury. He called to say he was looking forward to performing

the Christening. We were all a bit sad that
Dumbledore (Rowan Williams) wouldn't be
officiating, at the time, to be honest though.
One couldn't get a theological cigarette paper
between them, of course, but Dr Williams did
look like an Archbishop ought. "Facial hair,
that's the secret to a good Archbishop," the
Queen Mother, God rest her, always used to say.

Catherine stepped up the knitting in preparation
for the birth. She knitted everything from a duvet
cover to a crown and mace. We daren't mention it
to Charles; there's no telling what he'd do if he got
his hands on a crown, even a knitted one.

William said the antenatal classes went well.
They had considered a water birth so he could
have the RAF search and rescue helicopter
ticking over in the car park in case the waters get
choppy.

Finally, the moment came: a British winner at
Wimbledon, a second British triumph at the

Tour de France, winning the Ashes, unbroken sunshine and most important of all, a new Royal baby.

Don't let anyone say that defending the faith doesn't pay dividends.

The little sod kept us all waiting though (the baby, that is, not William). We were starting to wonder if Catherine had been bluffing about the whole expecting a baby thing. The DoE was convinced she'd been stuffing a pillow up her dress (he's always been suspicious since Edward pulled that trick in 1998. We waited a full ten months for the birth before we realised it was a phantom pregnancy – and only then because a corgi rather awkwardly pulled the pillow from Edward's maternity shirt).

Anyway, turns out that Catherine was determined to make William wait for his heir almost as long as he'd made her wait for an engagement ring.

One remembers it well. Only just gone to bed following the Tour de France celebration party at Windsor Castle ("Tour de Gin") when William called to say Catherine's waters had broken and they were hot-footing it in a Range Rover over to St Mary's. Mrs "Feet under the Palace table" Middleton called shortly afterwards to say she and Mr Middleton would be in his van and on their way to London just as soon as he managed to unhook the caravan and unload seven thousand boxes of party poppers, which was nice of them.

The birth was overseen by the Royal gynaecologist Alan Farthing, who called midmorning with an update that Catherine was doing absolutely fine but they'd had to give William gas and air and an epidural to keep him calm. At least that's what one thinks he said, one had actually had gas and air and an epidural to keep one calm at the time so wasn't entirely with it.

Traditionally of course, Royal births were witnessed by the Home Secretary and Archbishop of Canterbury but we've decided that they needn't bother this time, although William promised to text them a photo from his iPhone just to put their minds at rest on the strict understanding that they didn't upload it to Facebook. The last thing we need is a French magazine publishing them.

Mr Clegg called to ask if he were Deputy Royal Gynaecologist and to offer his Downing Street paddling pool in case a water birth were desired. One thanked him for the kind offer but said it was very much William and Catherine's wish that he got some use out of it himself whilst the weather was good. He seemed pleased, having just invested in an inflatable slide for it.

Ed Miliband got the wrong end of the stick and called to say he was delighted to hear Catherine had decided to join Labour. Didn't bother correcting him as one isn't entirely sure if he's old enough for the birds and the bees conversation.

Finally, the moment that the world had waited for: it was a prince. One was especially delighted – mainly because one had quite a few quid on it.

Third in line to the throne of sixteen sovereign nations, destined to become Head of the Armed Forces, Supreme Governor of the Church of England, Defender of the Faith, Pharaoh of Egypt and Captain America. God bless the little chap.

It wasn't long before one was well and truly in the grip of baby fever at Buckingham Palace. Within about seven minutes of them arriving, one was up to one's arse in baby clothes; it was as if one was starting up some kind of childcare establishment or something. To make it worse one had the Middletons staying for about six months after the birth. They really are quite bizarrely involved. One's surprised that Mrs "I've done this many times, allow me" Middleton didn't retrain as a midwife for the occasion.

Of course, in one's day, one simply gave birth to the heir, posed for the odd photo and essentially didn't see it until it was old enough to become a Duke or an Earl or something, but William and Catherine do insist on living a middle class life and have decided to be "fully involved" in the upbringing of their child.

As if it wasn't enough to bear that Mrs "Grandmother to a monarch in waiting" Middleton practically assumed all mothering responsibilities, Mr Middleton got in on the act as the self-appointed "Photographer Royal".

It was enough to drive one to distraction. One said to William when he bought him that ridiculous Polaroid camera for Christmas that it would lead to nothing but trouble. "Never shine light on magic," as the Queen Mother, God rest her, used to say.

One knew it wasn't going to turn out well
when Prince Harry got his hands on it after
Christmas lunch that year: the poor librarian
at Windsor Castle has been finding snapshots
of his "crown jewels" filed away in numerous
priceless first editions ever since. For one
terribly awkward moment she thought that she'd
found a previously undiscovered Leonardo da
Vinci anatomy study tucked into the back of
Pride and Prejudice. She only realised the truth
having become suspicious that Da Vinci didn't
tend to colour in his drawings ginger. The DoE
is convinced she'll never recover.

One wouldn't mind as much if Mr "call me
David Bailey" Middleton could actually frame a
decent shot, but out of the thousands he took of
the new happy family, only seven had William's
head intact.

It's actually still considered treason to cut off
the head of the second in line to the Throne,
in a photograph or otherwise, but after a long

conversation with the Attorney General, we decided it might not be strictly appropriate to prosecute.

Still, one has to work with what one's got. Sent the final selection over to Camilla for her opinion. She replied to say he looked adorable and so healthy and so much fun and that it really did make her wish she'd opted for a cocker spaniel too. Pointed out that it was Prince George that was the subject of the photo (though to be fair the framing did suggest otherwise) and she said he looked like a baby from what she could see through the sun glare and that was probably what the public would be expecting.

Not sure what it is about men and cameras. President Obama is the same; every time we have him over to Buckingham Palace he spends the entire time snapping away like some kind of Japanese tourist. The DoE is convinced he's on the payroll of the CIA.

Even Nick Clegg has caught the bug, although we've given him one of those toy pretend cameras that's essentially a mirror; poor chap can't work out why he can only take photos of his own face but it keeps him busy.

It's surprising really that Catherine and William aren't a bit more sensitive to cameras around the place as they are usually such a private couple. Although when you've had your principal assets plastered over the front of almost every continental magazine, there's probably not much else that the lens can reveal. Hopefully.

Prince Harry

His Royal Highness The Prince Henry of Wales.
Younger son of the Prince of Wales, third in
line to the throne of Great Britain and the
commonwealth realms, helicopter pilot and
nudist.

One remembers the day the nudism became
public: sitting down to breakfast at Balmoral
to find a blurred out but naked Prince Harry
staring back at one in the press from Las Vegas.
Nearly choked on one's bacon and egg sandwich!
Las Vegas!

If one has said it once, one has said it a million
times: just because nudity is the norm when
it comes to Royal BBQs, doesn't mean that
it's acceptable in Las Vegas hotel rooms, and
certainly not in the press. There is only one set

of crown jewels that should be seen in public on a regular basis and they're made from diamonds.

One has tried to explain to Harry that the problem with this kind of thing is that it snowballs into something altogether different. No sooner had his naked holiday been revealed in the press than Mrs "I've seen it all before and I do wish you'd call me Carole" Middleton called to say she and Mr Middleton had booked a caravan in a naturist resort in Bognor Regis and "would the DoE and I like to join her?" Accidentally agreed just to get her off the phone.

Really, one does one's best to fly the flag of monarchy but Prince Harry manages to steal the headlines with the Royal Arse. It's not even as if he were opening a hospital at the time or anything useful. There was a time when the headline "Royal Arse" meant Prince Andrew had been on a foreign visit of course but those days are long gone.

Thankfully one had a busy week at the time, what with a cabinet reshuffle and everything. (One has to admit; it's one of one's favourite things. One never tires of seeing the look of disappointment on the faces of sacked ministers.) Mr Clegg had called to say he wasn't involved in the reshuffle but that Mr Cameron had let him clear out the shed, which he was pleased about, so one was momentarily distracted from the Naked Prince.

Decided to get into the spirit of things and reshuffle Prince Harry to Afghanistan. It's a moment that every parent and grandparent fears, sending a red-haired relative to a place with strong sun and little shade, but he's got plenty of 'Factor 50' with him so he should be OK. Charles advised him to keep covered up, which, as we have seen, is easier said than done.

William was a bit upset that his little brother was seeing active service when he was "stuck in the arse-end of Wales rescuing things". Charles had to spend a good hour on the phone to him explaining why machine guns and missiles aren't strictly appropriate for a search and rescue helicopter unless you're flying over France regularly.

Harry seemed to enjoy it over in Afghanistan though. He sent a text shortly after he'd arrived saying that it was "absolutely sodding boiling, even without clothes on". We sent him over supplies once a month – just the essentials he might be missing from home – English breakfast tea, custard creams, Pippa Middleton; that sort of thing.

It was Christmas by the time he arrived back. Absolutely sodding freezing at Sandringham at the time. The DoE had been out all morning with an industrial flamethrower trying to clear the drive. It's impossible to walk the corgis in that weather; poor things were literally up to their arses in snow.

Prince Harry

Harry got something of a cold shock when
he arrived home. It came round quite quickly
actually; one couldn't believe how time flew by.
Seemed like only a few days ago he was in Vegas
and showing everybody his chopper.

We had him round for dinner to see how it had
all gone. He said it had been difficult fitting
in with the other soldiers when he's so clearly
different to them. One said that royalty is a cross
we have to bear and that being a Prince was a
privilege and not a burden and that he shouldn't
take it to heart that others saw him as different.
Turns out that he wasn't talking about the prince
thing at all – but about being the only nudist
in the army. Wasn't entirely sure what to say. It
is undeniably awkward. Still, be proud of the
crown and all that.

He seems to have had fun, although he's spent
the GDP of one of one's smaller overseas
territories on sunscreen since he's been out
there. Can't be too careful, what with being a

redhead and having skin only marginally less sensitive to the sun than that of a vampire – especially when he has a lot to cover.

He said he felt he managed to remain fairly incognito, though the Royal Standard flying from his helicopter and the National Anthem playing after each shot was a bit of a giveaway at times, apparently.

Of course, news of the Royal Baby broke whilst he was away. He was thrilled at the news and said it was good to see that William had been doing his duty over the last six months as well, and wondered if they were planning on calling the baby Harry or Harriet as a tribute to its war-hero uncle. One said one was sure they would give it some thought (they didn't).

He's a good boy at heart. Flew back from Afghanistan via France and Germany to fire a few warning shots at the Europeans before landing in the Downing Street back garden to remind Pinky and Perky (Cameron and Clegg) who's in charge.

The Middletons

When William decided to marry Catherine Middleton, we all thought it a bloody good idea. It's about time we had some new blood in the Royal Family (although Zara took the idea a bit far with that rugby chap but beggars can't be choosers). Unfortunately, with every new bride come in-laws or, in the case of the Middletons, outlaws.

One left it quite a while before agreeing to meet them but decided about a year before the wedding to invite them round for a family BBQ. Awkward is not the word.

Mr Middleton insisted on parking his Ford Sierra on the lawn and setting his picnic up in the boot, "tradition" or something. They'd brought a case of West Country cider with them

(the DoE says he used weaker antifreeze in the
Range Rover) and enough sausages to feed a
small Commonwealth nation. One did one's best
to make conversation but it really isn't that easy
when sitting in the grounds of Windsor Castle
answering questions like, "Have you been here
long?", "It must cost a pretty penny to heat?" and
comments such as "I had a friend with a castle
once, had a drawbridge and everything."

It's Mrs Middleton who wears the trousers
though. Or, more accurately, it's Mrs Middleton
who wears the jeans. There surely should be
some kind of law about a woman of a certain age
in skin tight denim. Andrew didn't know where
to look, although Camilla offered to show him.

Her first words were "Your Majesty, I do hope
you'll call me Carole. Can I call you Elizabeth?"
No. No, you can call one Your Majesty or Ma'am
(as in ham, not Marm as in palm) or you can
stay at home, one really doesn't mind which.
It's little wonder that Catherine has taken up

knitting so obsessively, the poor thing looked as if she wanted the ground to open up.

Still, in much the same way as an Englishman becomes used to living next to France, one has learned to cope with the new outlaws. Although one draws the line at holidays. They've got a caravan down in Sidmouth apparently and Mrs "call me Carole" Middleton is convinced that we'd all enjoy a long weekend on the coast. One really can think of nothing worse. And one doesn't care that "there's gourmet fish and chips and one of the best Cancer Research shops in Devon".

One doesn't see them often but Mr Middleton does like to call every couple of weeks and bring the DoE up to date on the latest products available via his online party business. One feels obliged to make the odd purchase and in just one year one has accumulated more Union Flag bunting and novelty party hats than comfortably fit in the garage. There's hardly enough room for a fleet of Bentleys.

There must be money in it though. Pippa Middleton, the younger daughter, has bought a book out with her top party tips. One can only imagine what such parties must actually be like. Harry's glued to it though. There's apparently a chapter on playing conkers, prompting him to text her asking if she'd like to play with his. He's still waiting for a reply.

There have only been two or three occasions when one has met Pippa Middleton, but she seems like a pleasant enough girl. Has a curious habit of saying, "smell you later" when she says goodbye. Although cannot for the life of one imagine how she managed to land a job writing for Waitrose Magazine. Surely not the Royal connection?

One can remember receiving the news. It was absolutely sodding freezing and one had been out with the corgis for their morning walk in the Buckingham Palace gardens (returned feeling like Sir Ranulph Fiennes). Hardly had chance to polish off a round of bacon and eggs when Mrs "I really do wish you would call me Carole" Middleton called to say that Pippa had got the job. What the hell happened to Delia?!

What is the world coming to? One had thought that Waitrose's famously sophisticated customers might have known how to pop a marshmallow on a skewer, or whatever it is she specialises in, but clearly not. Nearly withdrew the Royal Warrant, but one doesn't like to over-react.

Can't help but think that there is something more than a little strange in using Heston Blumenthal to encourage people to buy from Waitrose and then using Pippa Middleton to tell them how to cook it once they get it home. The DoE says it's like being sold a car by Jeremy Clarkson and taught to drive by Chris Huhne's ex-wife.

"Carole" was delighted though. Said she always knew that Pippa would make it as a kind of super-stylish Delia Smith. She used to throw

together fabulous meals for the whole family
when they were on holiday, apparently –
despite only having a gas fire in the caravan.
Remarkable.

Her repertoire is said to include:

1. How to put a party hat on without ruining
   one's hair
2. Warming marshmallows on a caravan gas
   fire
3. 101 things one can do with a tube of
   Pringles
4. Spam: the hidden gem in your cupboard
5. Meals to catch a second in line to the
   throne (still working on that one)

Of course, we're all hoping that Hilary Mantel
doesn't find out. If there's one thing worse than
offending her with the whole royalty concept
it's getting a shepherd's pie wrong, apparently.
And she's famed for her gravy in literary circles,
according to Camilla.

Waitrose was lucky to secure Miss Middleton in a way. She had originally agreed to write for Tesco magazine but had to pull out at the last minute, mainly due to her relative inexperience with horse meat recipes. Can't help but think that she should address that; it does somewhat limit retail food writing opportunities. Princess Anne could give her some tips. There's nothing that woman can't do with a horse.

Anyway, we're having them all over for New Year's Eve this year. William calls it "bonding", the DoE calls it "self-harm". But Mrs "it's New Year! Do call me Carole" Middleton has done a deal on a job-lot of party poppers and they're bringing some "Grab bags of wotsits", so it should be about as much fun as a night in with Gary Barlow. Let's face it, nothing can be worse than spending New Year in a giant dome with Mr and Mrs Blair.

Minor Royals

Most families have cousins or relatives whom we cannot change but do our best to avoid. In the Royal Family, we call these people "minor royals". It would of course be absolutely inappropriate to name them in these pages, but if you thought of The Duke and Duchess of Gloucester, The Duke and Duchess of Kent, and Prince and Princess Michael of Kent (all one's cousins and their wives), you wouldn't be far wrong.

That's not to say that minor royals are not hard working. Much like liberal democrats, they are very handy when there's no one proper for the job or when trying to make some kind of bizarre statement of bohemianism. As such, many organisations have named minor royals as patrons, presidents, rulers etc.

Of course, in days gone by, minor royals would be shipped off to run far-flung corners of the empire as viceroys, governor generals etc., although these days one wouldn't inflict them on even the most troublesome overseas territory. Except for France, where Princess Michael of Kent has been viceroy for approximately thirty years, although thankfully no one seems to have noticed. And Russia, where Prince Michael has been Tsar since the end of the Cold War.

Still, royal blood is thicker than water and all that. Once a year we have the bloody lot of them up to Balmoral for a family BBQ. The Duke and Duchess of Gloucester are usually first to arrive. He insists on driving all the way. It takes them about three weeks apparently, which is a long journey on a motorbike and sidecar. They seem to enjoy it though; the Duchess does love a bikers' café and she tells one there's a nice little place on the A1 that does a cracking full English with free tea refills if you arrive before 7am.

The 2011 BBQ was particularly memorable. It was just after Zara's marriage to Mr Tindall and they'd brought up half a wedding cake and a Range Rover full of Cava. All was as usual – Princess Michael of Kent was getting the BBQ going with a flamethrower and Edward was just taking the last batch of butterfly cakes out of the oven, when the Duchess of York appeared from behind a tree in a dress that looked like it had been fashioned from the Windsor Castle curtains and, swinging her knickers above her head, ran straight through the centre of the picnic and jumped into the lake.

You can imagine one's surprise. She hadn't been invited, for a start.

It was all very awkward, not least of all as her sudden appearance in the water nearly capsized Andrew's dinghy. Poor chap thought he was under attack from the Argentines. Luckily for her he didn't have his military issue water pistol with him; he'd have shot her.

The DoE fished her out with a carp net and we put her on the BBQ to dry off. Turns out the poor thing had been coming along every year and soaking up the atmosphere from behind a bush. It was all going quite well apparently until this year she was "stung in the arse by a bee the size of a sparrow".

Didn't have the heart to put her back behind the bush, what with the new beehive there and everything, so we let her stay for a burger. Edward spent the rest of the afternoon in total shock. He said he'll never look at that bush in the same light again.

Not sure what happened to Camilla, though. She was last seen covered in honey and streaking across the lawn with a cigar the size of a rolled up phonebook, shouting "sting me if you think you're fast enough".

Foreign Royal Families

Of course, before the world wars, a Royal Family ruled almost any country of note. It's a remarkably good system of Government, to be honest. Unfortunately, quite a few of them failed to wake up to the fact that letting the people think they were electing a Government was a much better way to avoid a revolution and many have fallen to the fashionable republics over the last 100 years.

Those that are left (one's own family aside) are essentially pretend or cartoon monarchs, designed to attract tourists etc. to the less interesting parts of the world (such as Europe and the Middle East).

To celebrate the Diamond Jubilee one had a few of them over for a light lunch of bacon

sandwiches at Windsor Castle. It's nice to catch
up with the extended family, most of whom
are descended from Queen Victoria, and share
the pain of dealing with the world's elected
representatives (or "idiots" as the DoE calls them).

The King of Bahrain arrived unfashionably early
at about 10am, which was a bit awkward as one
was still in one's dressing gown. Still, we sat him
in front of CBeebies with a slice of toast and a
glass of orange juice and he seemed quite happy.

No King and Queen of Spain, obviously. Poor
things couldn't afford the airfare. The Queen
of Spain did phone to explain that they were
"all a bit buggered" over there on the continent
at the time, which struck one as a bit of an
understatement. Still, one did promise to text
her if Phillip Schofield showed up – she loves
that man.

The King of Malaysia arrived via the tradesman's
entrance, something about tradition but one

wasn't really listening, to be honest. He'd apparently stayed on in London since the Royal Wedding the previous year – didn't see the point in flying back and forth. Apparently he finds ruling via Skype more than effective, which is how one tends to rule in Australia and New Zealand, come to think of it.

Lunch started promptly with a quick round up of world news and a bit of teasing of Charles that he's still not King. The pain was shared by the King of Thailand's son, Crown Prince Vajiralongkorn and his wife Princess Srirasm (who, incidentally, is never seen without an enormous cigar – and one's talking marrow size), who've been waiting to accede since 1946.

Prince Albert II of Monaco got the post-lunch game of charades off to a good start. It took surprisingly long for anyone to guess what he was miming, considering that it was "Queen". It was the Freddie Mercury impression that did it in the end.

Edward always gets excited at these Royal gatherings. Hadn't seen this many Queens in one room since Elton John's birthday party, apparently. He's particularly fond of King Abdullah of Saudi Arabia, who's teaching him how to play the drums.

Of course, it's always a bit awkward when one meets with other Sovereign Monarchs. One tries not to make them feel inferior about only ruling one country each, but there's no hiding the fact that one is head of state in sixteen sovereign nations and head of the commonwealth of many more. As the DoE says, "you rule". Indeed.

2
Politics

Mrs Thatcher

There are two things about Mrs Thatcher that stand out amongst one's other Prime Ministers: she was a woman and she drank neat anti-freeze with ice and a slice. On this account, the DoE and I decided to go along in person to her funeral to pay our respects.

It's not often that one loses a prime minister. (Having said that, we did think we'd lost Mr Cameron at Sandringham one Christmas: the DoE was convinced he'd fallen down a disused mineshaft or something but turns out the poor chap got stuck in the downstairs loo. Was in there for about two days before anyone had noticed he'd gone, apparently, which was a bit awkward.)

Had no idea what to wear. Mrs Thatcher was always very keen on the full state regalia but one couldn't help but think that a crown was a little too sparkly for a solemn occasion. She specifically requested that she was not to lie in state (never did like lying down on the job), but we got a few thousand troops to line the streets all the same.

One had one's ups and downs, as one has with all prime ministers, of course. But one can't help but think that it is a little strange without Mrs Thatcher around. The foreigners were petrified of her, of course.

In fact, the only way we've managed to keep the North Koreans under control this long is because they think she's still in government. And in a manner of speaking, of course, she still is. Let's hope that no one has mentioned that Ronald Reagan is no longer around. There's no telling what they might do.

Say what you like about Mrs Thatcher, she did have the courage of her convictions. Her private secretary once told one that they had driven for miles in the wrong direction after taking the wrong exit on the M4 with her insisting that she was "not for turning"; apparently they nearly ended up in Swindon, which is a position no politician wants to be in. Essentially the political opposite of Mr Clegg, who has made something of a career out of it.

President Hollande of France called to give his condolences, which came as a bit of a shock. If there was one thing Mrs Thatcher could not stand, it was the French. It's a little known fact that the Falklands task force was in fact heading to Paris when the Argentines invaded, and was diverted at the last minute to the South Atlantic. One week later and she would have been flying the Union Flag from the top of the Eiffel Tower.

One thing we had in common, of course, was a handbag. The contents of one's handbag are a state secret but one can reveal that Mrs Thatcher's contained: a lump of coal, Arthur Scargill's left testicle, lipstick, the remote control for Ronald Reagan, and a brick (made heavier for bashing her cabinet colleagues with, apparently).

If there were one thing that annoyed the nation (miners aside) more than anything else, however, it was her incessant use of the Royal "we". As one reminded her on more than one occasion, there are only two Queens in this country, one is one and the other is Elton John.

Still, at least she made an impression. Mr Cameron often worries if people would remember him more than thirty years after he had taken office. One can't help but wonder if anyone remembers Mr Cameron 30 minutes after he has left the room.

David Cameron

The Right Honourable David Cameron MP, Prime Minister of the United Kingdom, First Lord of the Treasury, Minister for the Civil Service and Leader of the Conservative Party. Or Zippy, as we call him.

Mr Cameron is actually one's 11th Prime Minister (12th if you include Gordon Brown but no one does). When he was born in 1966 one had already been in charge for fourteen years – as one reminds him once a week at his audience with one.

There are two types of Prime Minster: those who know their place and those who think we're friends. Mr Cameron is sadly the second. He insists, *insists*, on asking one over for lunch as if one is some Tory Party donor or something.

After months of refusing, the DoE had (what he thought was a safe) bet with him that it would rain right through the Olympics and said we would go for lunch at Downing Street if it didn't, and so sadly that's what we had to do.

Mr Cameron had invited Gordon Brown, Tony Blair and John Major along (safety in numbers and all that). Mrs Blair was unfortunately unable to make it due to an ongoing knee problem, which makes it virtually impossible for her to curtsey, and also due to not being invited. Mrs Thatcher, whilst technically alive at the time, was also absent, having given up public duties in 1983.

Mr Blair was looking ridiculously tanned. It never ceases to amaze one how someone with his popularity (or lack of it) can smile so much. He asked if one had enjoyed his memoirs and one assured him that they'd taken pride of place in the Royal Library (as a doorstop – one didn't know if they should be filed under humour or fiction). The DoE asked him how saving the world was a coming along, Mr Blair said it was a slow process but he felt he was getting there. Mr Cameron chipped in that it sounded similar to his experience with the Olympics.

It must have been quite a novelty for Mr Cameron, having a lunch guest that hadn't made a sizable donation to the Conservative Party in order to be there. The DoE asked if Andy Coulson or Rebekah Brooks would be joining us but apparently they were otherwise engaged. The DoE said he thought they might have a chance to dine at one's pleasure soon.

Lunch was rather good, to be fair, although the first course didn't arrive – something to do with G4S being responsible for the delivery, one wasn't really listening to be honest.
Mr Major said it brought back memories of a curry he'd had in the White Drawing Room and the DoE asked if he was talking about Edwina.

Couldn't help feel sorry for Mr Brown. He'd hardly had chance to unpack his suitcase, he was here for such a short time. Mr Cameron let him have a sit at the Prime Minister's desk one last time and there was an awkward moment when he refused to leave (again).

Mr Clegg didn't join us at lunch but he seemed to be enjoying himself outside in the Downing Street paddling pool. Mr Cameron said he was "keeping him covered in 'Factor 50' sunscreen to stop him getting burned, but you just can't keep him out of the water when it's sunny". Slightly traumatic moment when he dropped his Etch-a-Sketch into the pool, thus practically bringing the Liberal Democrats to a virtual standstill, but Mr Blair gave it a shake (the Etch-a-Sketch, not Mr Clegg) and calm was restored. He was back on form in no time and spent the rest of the afternoon squirting Mr Brown through the window with a water pistol.

Group therapy session over, one issued a quick

motivational bollocking for political decision-making past, present and future and we jumped in the Bentley and headed back to Buckingham Palace for a G4S (gin, 4 shots) in the garden.

Nick Clegg

The Right Honourable Nick Clegg MP, Leader of the Liberal Democrat Party and work experience student at Downing Street.

Nick Clegg is David Cameron's work experience student. He was originally only meant to stay for one day ("Bring a Liberal Democrat to Work Day") in 2010 but has stayed around ever since. Still, his drawings and paintings have certainly brightened up the Downing Street downstairs loo and Mr Cameron says it is nice to have a little person around the place; helps him focus on providing better education in the future, etc.

Mr Clegg can most often be found in the Downing Street garden, where he has a sandpit, paddling pool and swingball. Poor chap hasn't

managed to get the hang of the swingball,
despite many years of practice. Can't seem to
understand why when he hits the ball hard
it ends up coming back round and smacking
him in the back of the head. The DoE says it's
become a metaphor for his political policies,
which have a habit of doing the same.

During Cabinet meetings, Mr Clegg takes notes
on his Government-issue Etch-a-Sketch. It all
generally goes well, although we had a bit of an
issue when the knob fell off during a discussion
about renegotiating our place in Europe, which
was both unfortunate and ironic. Mr Clegg
immediately called for help on his mobile phone
but sadly was unable to get a signal, mainly
because it's a Fisher-Price phone.

He is very good with technology though,
considering his age. He very quickly learned
how to FaceTime on Mr Cameron's iPad, so
much so that he demanded one of his own.
Due to austerity measures, we got him a mirror

instead but he does have a lot of fun video-calling himself.

After his success in the television leadership debates before the 2010 general election, Mr Clegg decided he was a dab hand at "mass debating" (the DoE says he has a point but one's not sure they are both thinking along the same lines). Unfortunately this proved untrue when he agreed to debate with the UKIP leader Nigel Farage on Britain's place in Europe, live on BBC2 in what was trailed at a sequel to the Chuckle Brothers.

It was all a bit embarrassing, to be honest. In the pressure of the moment, Mr Clegg forgot all the lines that Angela Merkel had written for him. She was so angry. Still, could have been worse, it's not as if anyone was actually watching.

Mr Clegg's work experience comes to an end in 2015, when he and the Liberal Democrat Party will cease to exist.

Ed Miliband

The Right Honourable Ed Miliband MP, Leader of Her Majesty's Most Loyal Opposition.

One has very few memories of Ed Miliband, mainly because one can never understand a sodding word he's saying. The DoE says that the only Miliband worth having in the Palace is the Glenn Miller Band.

Ed, of course, shot to fame whilst standing on his brother David's head in the Labour leadership election. Mr Cameron says that is exactly the problem with the Alternative Vote: everyone votes and elects someone no one actually wanted. Which explains why the Liberal Democrats are so attached to the concept.

Not sure why he decided to pursue a career in politics, to be honest. He seemed to be having some success as Mr Bean and really ought to have stuck at something he was good at. One thought his performance at the London Olympic Closing Ceremony particularly enjoyable.
Say what you like about Ed Miliband, he is effortlessly funny. Although one isn't entirely sure he tries to be.

He was of course initially destined for a life as a Tube train driver, where it was hoped that he'd rise to lead the RMT Union. However, this sadly didn't have quite as good prospects for drawing generously from the public purse so as to please his staunchly socialist father, so he went into the Labour Party instead. Say what you like about those socialists but they are always head of the champagne queue at one's garden parties.

Still, it's nice for Mr Clegg to have someone his own age to play hopscotch with in Parliament. Although it is a worry that one day the British public might elect the two of them by mistake. One really can't imagine asking them to form a Government together. The DoE says he wouldn't ask them to form a conga.

Nigel Farage

Where the sodding hell did Nigel Farage come
from?! He's not even a Member of Parliament.
One day one is enjoying a fairly benign two-
party system (three if you include the Liberal
Democrats, which no one ever does) and the
next Farage is on the TV every week. The DoE is
convinced that the BBC have got him on some
kind of Question Time block booking. And why
does he always have a pint of beer in his hand? Is
he a landlord?

Despite winning the 2014 European elections,
the poor chap seems to be a little misguided
about Europe. One doesn't have the heart to
break it to him that after World War II it was
decided that despite having won, it would seem
a little over the top for the British to declare
Sovereign rule across the continent and so

we decided instead to administer it via a new organisation, called the European Union. Based the whole thing in Brussels so no one would notice, but it's essentially been under British control ever since.

Ironically, the Europeans would love Britain to withdraw; they've been trying to persuade us for years by not voting for us in the Eurovision Song Contest. But it is a system that works rather well. We call the shots; the Germans pay the bills.

Still, anyone who annoys the hell out of Mr Cameron can't be all bad in one's book. Thinking of elevating him to the House of Lords, just to see the look on Mr Cameron's face at the thought of having to call him "Your Lordship". Must get onto that.

The State Opening of Parliament

One's favourite political moment of the year.
All the MPs and Lords assemble to pay homage
to one in all one's finery and to hear the
Government's plans for the parliamentary year
ahead. One says "plans", they're actually more
like the collective imagination of the cabinet
of the time. If they were truthful, they'd say
something like "One's Government will spend
the year dreaming up new ways to part one's
subjects from their hard earned cash and to
curtail their freedom in the name of freedom
itself," but that's generally felt to be a bit
unpalatable for the electorate.

Winston Churchill used to write the best
speeches, of course. In those days, before TV
cameras in the House, one could have a bit of
fun and read them out in assorted accents. One's

Gandhi impression had the Lords in tears of laughter once. Those were the days.

These days it's all a bit more sombre. There's nothing like the cold glare of the media to take the fun out of something. We still do the pomp, though, much to the Liberal Democrats' disappointment. They have a manifesto commitment to "make Britain so boring it can quietly slide onto the continent without anyone noticing" apparently. Still, thankfully they haven't much chance of ever being in power (although, as one writes, we're letting them pretend. One wasn't sure but David Cameron thought it would "be a laugh" and Nick Clegg was desperate to do some work experience).

The Green Party do like the State Opening though – they see one's journey up the Mall in a horse-drawn carriage as an "environmental statement". One hasn't mentioned that the return journey is by six-litre petrol Bentley.

The crown arrives in its own little carriage, which confuses some of the tourists who think that they've caught a glimpse of the top of one's head as it drives past. One may be on the shorter side of life but one does manage to see out of windows, one can assure you.

It's all a bit of a ritual when one gets into Parliament. One doesn't enter the House of Commons, not because it's independent or anything like that, but because all those MPs squashed into one little space does rather insult one's sensitive sense of smell. Black Rod – the DoE thought for years his name was actually Rod but has recently discovered it's the name of his office. He said that explains why his rod isn't black – goes and gets them by banging on the door, in much the same way as one wakes up Edward in the mornings.

2012's State Opening was particularly traumatic. Thought for a second about abolishing the lot and putting the DoE in charge but thought it'd be unfair to bring Mr Clegg's work experience to such an abrupt end.

Arrived on the dot and went up to the Robe Room to get one's swag on. The DoE had brought along a party hat, which he thought would make a change from the usual crown thing, but we decided on balance it might be a progressive step too far and that we'd stick with the traditional.

Read out the rubbish that Cameron had jotted down and got out of there faster than a corgi that'd been stung in the arse. At least one would have got out of there if one hadn't been trapped in a lift for about ten minutes, which was deeply awkward. One was up and down like Cameron's poll ratings before finally arriving back at the carriage for the ride back to the palace.

Could have been worse, could have been in there with Mr Cameron.

Chairing a Cabinet Meeting

One generally leaves pretending to run the country to politicians, of course, but during one's Diamond Jubilee year one thought it about time one took personal charge of the Government so popped over to Downing Street to chair the Cabinet meeting and do a spot of ministerial ego-realigning.

Did consider wearing the full State regalia, including the Imperial State Crown, but the DoE thought they'd be intimidated enough having their Sovereign Lady and undoubted Queen in the room without having to look at a few million pounds worth of diamonds at the same time.

Mr Cameron had rolled out the red carpet, bless him. Although quite frankly it was all a bit downhill from there. Does Mrs Cameron not own a Dyson? One was ankle-deep in dust within about 30 seconds of walking through the front door.

The assembled Ministers lined up to say good morning, including Mr Gove who is sporting some new glasses that make him look like some kind of 1950s underworld boss. George Osborne "joked" that there's not as much gold in Downing Street as one encountered at the Bank of England and then proceeded to roar with laughter like a man possessed.

Quick smile for the cameras and then down to business. One started by holding a quick team building exercise whereby each Minister took turns to explain why one shouldn't immediately dismiss the Government and establish direct rule. Not entirely sure what Eric Pickles said, partly because one was talking over him at the time and mainly because he spent the entire meeting trying to talk with about seven custard creams in his mouth.

Amazing: every single Liberal Democrat Minister drinks herbal tea. Mr Cable said it was a sign of progressive Government and that he was keen to embrace change. One said that unless they got the economy in shape pronto one would be embracing a progressive change of Government.

No idea whom one had to knight to get a decent earl grey and rich tea biscuit in that sodding place. Honestly, it was like brunch at the Middletons'.

We did a quick brainstorm of policy ideas for the New Year, which Mr Clegg captured on a flip chart with his crayons, and one explained that for austerity reasons one would be freezing ministerial salaries between now and approximately the end of recorded time. They seemed to take it well.

Mr Cameron ended the meeting by expressing his congratulations on the occasion of one's

Diamond Jubilee and presenting one with a
gift from the whole cabinet: a set of placemats.
Placemats. Sixty sodding placemats.

What part of "Bentley" wasn't clear? Or, for
that matter, "Royal Yacht"? Almost fifty happy
years one spent sailing around the world firing
warning shots at various smaller nations and
the closest thing we've got to a boat these days is
Andrew's inflatable dinghy on the Buckingham
Palace fish pond. It's a national disgrace.

Was just about to hot-foot it back to the Palace
when Mr Hague insisted on showing me his
office across the road in the Foreign Office. One
couldn't refuse as he was so excited, so off we
went to meet an endless line of officials telling
one how well he was doing. It was like some
kind of parents' evening in hell.

Still, not all was lost. As one was about to jump
in the car, he announced that he'd bought the
Antarctic for one, which he was going to name

"Queen Elizabeth Land". That's more like it. A little cold, but better than a set of placemats.

Got back to the Palace and updated the DoE on the news. He said that "Queen Elizabeth Land" sounded like a theme-park but was chuffed all the same.

Put the placemats on eBay (buyer collects) and visited the second cabinet of the day: the gin cabinet.

Political Scandal

There are two types of scandal that the British love: A Royal scandal and a political scandal. These are otherwise known as scandals one does not love and scandals one does.

Political scandals literally make one's year. Heaven knows what we're going to do for news now that the *News of the World* has closed. One was hacking their phone for years; honestly it was better than listening to the Archers. One always tries to look surprised when the Prime Minister comes round to officially notify one though. It's not good form to know whom ministers are sleeping with before the press or the Prime Minister.

What one simply cannot understand is why on earth politicians take such chances. One can understand how occasionally they succumb to love, but Chris Huhne practically ruined an otherwise promising political career (if such a thing is possible in the Liberal Democrats) to avoid a speeding fine. Although every cloud does have a silver lining: one managed to persuade his ex-wife to pay the 500 years of parking fines one incurred when they found Richard III buried under a car park.

The expenses scandal was the last straw though. One was absolutely amazed by what the greedy sods were claiming. A duck house, for Christ's sake. Do they think one is made of money?! One has since been signing their expense claims off personally. And a taxi from Downing Street to Parliament is not a legitimate expense, Mr Cameron. One doesn't care if it was raining and you had your best suit on!

Audiences with Prime Ministers

Audiences with Prime Ministers are one's weekly chance to re-align the ego of one's most senior politician. It's a full and frank exchange of views, in that they come in with their view and leave with one's view.

Of course, prime ministerial audiences have changed through the years. Queen Victoria used to insist her Prime Ministers remained standing for the entire time, and considering she used to have them over for about twelve hours at a time, it was a little uncomfortable to say the least.

One's father, King George VI, was a little more understanding and gave the poor chap a chair. Of course it was World War II at the time, so there was a lot to talk about.

One's first Prime Minister was Winston Churchill. Terrific man. Although he did insist on addressing one as if one were a public meeting. He was a great favourite of papa's, of course. The two of them having won a world war and all that; it's good bonding.

Sir John Major was nice. Used to love a custard cream, one seems to remember. Never expected (or wanted) to become prime minister, of course, and used to end each Audience in tears and pleading with one not to send him back to the "bastards" in Downing Street. Bit awkward. Really, one didn't know where to look. There was more than one occasion when one would have been lost for words, if one had actually let the poor man stay instead of having him ejected by a passing footman.

Of all one's prime ministers, Harold Wilson is a bit of a favourite. There's something deeply refreshing about someone who can talk for ten minutes about how they fundamentally disagree with the trappings of wealth and power and then ask for a Polaroid of themselves.

The most traumatic were those with Mr Blair. Absolutely insisted on bringing Mrs Blair with him, although one insisted she wait outside in the car. He used to spend half the time telling one about what a wonderful job he was doing and the other half moaning about Mr Brown. Ironically, audiences with Mr Brown were exactly the same, although he spent half the time moaning about himself and biting his nails (vile habit; biting the nails that is, not being Mr Brown. Although that is bad enough).

Audiences are on a strict timetable and after thirty-five minutes, one presses a little button which opens up a trap door beneath the Prime Minister's chair, through which they drop down a tunnel and out of the side of the palace into a waiting car to take them back to Downing Street. Can't have them hanging around for too long. One's got an Empire to run.

Abu Hamza and the Home Office

It does sometimes come as a shock to the British people that their ever-loving and undoubted Queen should offer words of advice (direction) to ministers of the crown, but when the BBC's Frank Gardner spilled the beans about one's attempts to deport Abu Hamza, it caused a bit of the stir in the more colourful topped newspapers.

Frank sodding Gardner. Should have known one couldn't trust him to keep it quiet. "Don't worry Your Majesty, what's said on tour, stays on tour." Whatever. Well, he can forget ever receiving another honour. In fact, one's seriously considering having him downgraded from an OBE to a Blue Peter Badge.

One doesn't usually let one's guard down but one was holding a little cocktail party for members of the press at Buckingham Palace and, quite frankly, one was approximately three-quarters full of gin by about 11pm when Gardner cornered one against a giant vase.

The DoE says it's just as well the whole conversation didn't come out. One had mentioned Hamza (Captain Hook, as Camilla calls him) in passing. Being a caring, sharing sort of a Queen, one's closely interested in the safely of one's subjects. And one really can't have pirates roaming around the place. One has enough of that in the Caribbean.

One happened to mention to Mr Gardner that one was making a little list of people to be deported for the sake of public safety/sanity/happiness, etc. Looked back in one's diaries to find the top contenders:

1. Abu Hamza
2. Mr and Mrs Blair
3. Cliff Richard

4. Paul McCartney
5. Richard Madeley
6. Everyone who has ever appeared on Big Brother (including "celebrity" version)
7. Lord Sugar
8. Members of Parliament (past and present)

Camilla called to say she'd be quite happy to see Hamza off the premises personally and that she could do with a trip to the US as she wanted to pick up some gin and cigarettes in duty free on the way. She thought Hamza might be useful to carry the bags, what with the hook and all.

The problem that global monarchs such as oneself face when it comes to deporting people is that there are very few places one can put them where one isn't actually head of state.

Called Obama, he said they'd take Hamza at a push but the Blairs were a definite no-no. Russia said they'd take McCartney and Cliff Richard on strict understanding they could hand them back if they ever attempted to sing in Russian. Channel 5 said they'd be willing to take the Big Brother contestants on condition they could broadcast 24/7 repeats (which is fine as no one would see them).

Absolutely no one willing to take MPs, Lord Sugar or Richard Madeley. Very frustrating.

3
Celebrity

Freddie Mercury

One doesn't have many regrets in life. Not
knighting Freddie Mercury is one of them.
Every year, on the anniversary of his death, one
throws a little Queen Karaoke Party at Windsor
Castle. The DoE usually comes as Freddie
Mercury circa 1986 but Edward prefers to go for
the 1977 look. Thinks the sequined jumpsuit is
more his thing and all that.

Camilla is usually first up with her rendition
of 'We Will Rock You', which always gets the
party started, followed swiftly by Charles with
'Another One Bites the Dust', which he dedicates
to each year that passes without him ascending
the Throne. It was Catherine's first Queen
Karaoke last year of course, and she did a rather
good job of 'Bohemian Rhapsody' to be fair to
her, with Princesses Beatrice and Eugenie on

backing vocals. She'd knitted everyone their own Freddie Mercury jumper as a special surprise, bless her. The Duchess of York used to do a rather good 'I Want to Break Free' but obviously hasn't been around much since actually breaking free. One finishes proceedings with one's own version of 'Killer Queen', which is live streamed to Heads of Government around the world as something of a warning.

It's a little known fact that the only way one manages to get through Royal Variety Performances without ordering the RAF to flatten the bloody place is by watching Queen concerts on a little screen hidden in the Royal Box. The cameras often cut to one to show one is having a good time but that's generally because Freddie Mercury is mid-'Bohemian Rhapsody' and nothing to do with the assembled morons on stage at the Palladium or wherever we are. Still, the Show Must Go On.

Gary Barlow

Gary Barlow. Gary sodding Barlow. The Bob the Builder of music, as the DoE calls him.

According to Edward, there was a time when Mr Barlow was the boy-band member that no one fancied. But give it about twenty years, a stone more weight and some designer stubble and it's like being reborn, apparently. We were just daring to hope that Elton John had moved into semi-retirement when along comes Gary Barlow to pick up where he left off.

One should never have agreed to him organising one's Diamond Jubilee concert. Honestly, one has never encountered such an obsessive man. He wanders around with his little clipboard and tape measure with a pencil behind his ear like some sort of tradesman. No idea what he was actually doing – and more to the point, neither did he.

It's always the same story when one gets a man in. They're full of optimism and no problem is too big until they actually start work. "Oooo that's going to cost more than I first thought, yer maj," he used to say.

And the tea. One has never known anyone drink as much tea. And when he wasn't drinking it, he was pissing like a corgi. Honestly, one couldn't get through a single conversation without him nipping off to use the "facilities".

God only knows how he's turned into such a star. The DoE says there's nothing you can't do with a regional accent, these days. There was a time when a Manchester accent practically qualified you for disability benefits but now it's like an automatic pass for TV work.

What's most bizarre is the incessant humming of Robbie Williams' songs. It really is very strange. Three months he was at the Palace every day preparing for one's concert. If one ever hears 'Let meeeeeeeeee entertain you…' again, it'll be too soon. He says he can't stand Robbie Williams when one asks him, but Edward is sure he caught a glimpse of a photo of him in Barlow's wallet.

Sadly the concert wasn't the end of it. If he isn't popping in for a "cuppa" he's texting the Royal iPhone: "Are you watching me on *X Factor*, yer maj?", "Doing a job round the corner, can I pop in?", "Are you still awake?", "I miss you", "All I do each night is pray, hoping that I'll be a part of you again someday", that kind of thing. Seriously considering changing one's number.

John Major, who pops over on a Saturday morning for a custard cream and to watch *Saturday Kitchen* with one, is convinced he's after a knighthood. Cliff Richard was exactly the same. If he wasn't popping up at every single national event singing 'Congratulations' he was doing a rain dance at the Wimbledon Tennis Championships. One had to give in eventually. It was more than a nation could take.

Still, all that prancing about at the Palace doesn't get you out of paying your tax bill, Mr Barlow. That little scheme he was paying into was decidedly dodgy. The DoE got straight on the phone and explained that one "wants your tax, wants your tax, wants your tax for good". One thinks he got the gist. The cheeky bugger.

H

In the scheme of
has made more o
Queen than one h
awkward actually.
popped into Pizza ~~~~~~ for a sloppy giuseppe
and spent about an hour signing autographs for
about seven hundred tourists who thought one
was her.

Helen Mirren was of course an unknown actress
(if you don't count *Prime Suspect*, as no one
really does) before portraying one in *The Queen*
– a wildly fictitious film about New Labour
saving the British Monarchy from disaster,
loosely based on one of Mr Blair's recurring
dreams, apparently. And since then she's made
something of a career out of it. The DoE says
she's more one than one these days.

it was about time that one
ion and sloped off to watch
Audience, although quite frankly
eated so far back one was practically
rey. It was like being a Beckham at a Royal
edding.

The whole thing is set in the Audience Room
of Buckingham Palace, save for a short stint at
Balmoral, and on the whole they seem to have
got it pretty spot on. Although to be perfectly
honest, audiences with Prime Ministers are not
actually in the Audience Room but are in fact
held in one's private sitting room, where one can
be close to the state papers (*Racing Post*) and the
Great Seal of the Realm (gin).

The thought of two and a half hours of watching
one's prime ministerial audiences dramatised
filled one with dread, one doesn't mind telling
you. The real things are traumatic enough.
But by the end one was quite tempted to hire
Mirren to stand in for one like some kind of

body double – would save one having to speak to Prime Ministers and she does seem to enjoy getting all dressed up like that.

Still, it does come in handy to have a body double to send on official visits to France, and she always brings back a boot full of lager and fags for The Duchess of Cornwall.

Hilary Mantel

What is it with authors? They write a couple of best-selling novels and all of a sudden they've got an opinion on everything. To be honest, one wasn't entirely sure if Hilary Mantel's comments on royalty and Catherine were real or fiction.

Had initially thought she was pitching a new book wherein a plastic princess is a model for rags, as painfully thin as anyone could wish, without the risk of the emergence of character, or something like that. Sounded like a Nick Clegg biography quite frankly, give or take the bit about being thin.

Still, sounded very interesting and exciting, one must say. Thought it were quite a departure for Ms Mantel, who thus far has based her books on facts. Turns out that it wasn't a pitch for a new book at all but an observation of celebrity culture and how difficult it is to be a royal woman in the 21st century.

Got her on the phone quick smart to explain herself. She said she'd been quoted out of context; the *Daily Mail* had sensationalised the whole thing, thus proving her point etc., etc. Wasn't quite able to hear the end of her explanation, partly because one had an urgent afternoon appointment with the *Racing Post*. But can't help but wonder what she thought the media would do with her comments, if not sensationalise them.

Mrs "both of our families have been attacked in the media, I do hope you'll call me Carole" Middleton called to say she was shocked and saddened, especially as she's just had her new caravan named Wolf Hall. Turns out she hadn't got much further than the front page of the *Daily Mail* and said it all made a bit more sense when she'd read the whole thing.

Catherine was more reflective, saying it made a nice change for her to be in the media with her clothes on. William was a bit upset though. If one were Ms Mantel, one would be looking out for low flying RAF search and rescue helicopters for the next few decades.

The whole episode did give one an idea for a book of one's own though. In it, an author writes a couple of enormously successful novels before offending the Queen and spending the rest of her days decorating the basement of the Tower of London with the *Daily Mail*, wallpaper-paste that doesn't quite stick and Paul McCartney playing on loop. The DoE thinks it's a potential Booker Prize winner.

David Beckham

Rumour has it that David Beckham used to be a football player, although quite frankly one had no idea until he announced his retirement. The DoE was convinced he were only famous since marrying into the Spice Girls.

More shocking was that he actually gave the resignation statement himself. One had actually absolutely no idea he could talk. But, as the ex-Queen of the Netherlands always used to say, if you can't speak out when you're throwing in the towel, when can you?

Apparently David Beckham had not really wanted to go at all but, following Sir Alex Ferguson's retirement, they couldn't find anyone to operate him. Sooty had much the same problem when Matthew Corbett retired.

Still, it'll give him more time to spend
supporting those whom are desperately short of
food, or Victoria, as one believes she is called.

It must be very difficult for Victoria, of course.
Her husband's retirement from football will
be met with universal sadness and praise for a
long and successful career; her retirement from
music was met with a spontaneous outpouring
of joy and relief the world over.

Mr Beckham has been a wonderful ambassador
for this country. He made 115 appearances
for England and 394 for Manchester United,
winning six Premier League titles and the
Champions League (apparently, one didn't see
all/many/any of them, one has to admit).

One was a little disappointed that he arrived
late for the Olympic Opening Ceremony
though. Having to resort to tearing up the River
Thames in a speedboat and holding some kind
of massive cigar is a little unbecoming, and one

says that as a monarch who arrived at the very same event by jumping from a helicopter.

Prince Charles didn't take the news well. Every time the poor chap hears "shock retirement" on the news he gets his hopes up. He texted to say retirement was very fashionable and how nice it was for David Beckham to move aside to give younger people a chance. One didn't reply.

He (likes to think he) has become quite good friends with Prince William over these last few years though. They have quite a lot in common, such as the sheer international embarrassment of trying to secure Seb Blotter (or whatever his name is) to let England host the World Cup only to be made to look like complete idiots. Can't blame them for trying though. The DoE said it was the only chance we'd have of getting that particular trophy on British soil for the next thousand years.

Yes, the football world will miss David Beckham. But let's hope for all our sakes he doesn't embark on a new career to which he is completely unsuited. Like public speaking.

4

Royal Travel and
Foreign Affairs

State Visits

In the world of so-called "soft power", there is no greater weapon than a British State Visit. One regularly nips off around the globe projecting majesty and generally intimidating the world's smaller nations on official State Visits, but being invited to spend a couple of days with one in the United Kingdom is generally considered the pinnacle of any lesser head of state's time in office.

Had the Amir of the State of Kuwait over for a few days in 2012. Sent Charles and Camilla to go and collect him and give him a lift to Windsor Castle. Camilla texted to say he thought Charles was a cab driver. Awkward.

Anyway, he arrived at Windsor on time and we had the customary carriage journey up the hill to the Castle. The poor chap hadn't come prepared for the weather and got absolutely sodding soaked, although he was very nice about it. One laid on a few custard creams and a pot of tea and Camilla gave him the once-over with a hairdryer to dry him off a bit.

Ed Miliband popped round to say hello. The Amir had specifically asked to see him, which Mr Miliband took as a great honour. We didn't mention that it was because the Amir thought he was Mr Bean (he's got the complete series on DVD apparently). Still, in the circumstances, they appeared to get on famously. The DoE said it was probably because neither of them speaks very good English.

Customary State Banquet in the evening. Dumbledore (the outgoing Archbishop of Canterbury) was there, along with Thelma and Louise (Mr Cameron and Mr Clegg) and Bungle (Boris Johnson). We usually try and get the dinner over and done with quickly and move on to the State Karaoke. The Amir is a dead ringer for Mika, apparently.

Managed to find time to give Mr Cameron a quick call mid-afternoon to deliver a thermonuclear bollocking that his Work Programme had not yet produced results. He said the Coalition had created jobs for many people who had previously experienced years of unemployment, such as the Liberal Democrats. Told him he was on probation until the end of recorded time or until the electorate kicks him out on his arse, whichever is sooner.

America

As Queen of America, one regularly pops over to see how they are getting on, provide regal leadership and direction and reassess their limited independence. One's first visit was in October 1957, visiting President Eisenhower.

He was a strange chap. Dwight David Eisenhower, or Dwight D. Eisenhower, as he liked to be known. Never trust a man who insists on giving his middle initial out to all and sundry. It speaks of a deep-rooted self-loathing, in one's experience. You never see one signing letters "Elizabeth A. M. Windsor", do you?

One had been on the throne for five years in 1957 and thought it were high time one hotfooted it over the Atlantic to check on the colonials. Winston Churchill was particularly

keen for one to make the visit. Eisenhower
owed him about 200 quid from a card game
they'd played during World War II, when he
was a General in the American division of the
British Army, and Churchill was having an awful
problem getting him to pay up. That's the thing
about Americans: bad payers.

It wasn't the best of state visits, to be honest. It's
a little known fact that Eisenhower had very
little taste in food. He said he'd booked a rather
nice Turkish restaurant for one's first night,
which turned out to be essentially a table in a
takeaway. All very strange.

It was twenty odd years before one ventured
back, to see President Ford in 1976. One has
absolutely no memory of him whatsoever,
although the DoE says he was very nice for
someone named after a car.

Yes, one does try to keep the American trips
down to a minimum. It's an accepted historical

fact that the early British settlers who discovered America tried to keep it a secret for years, and frankly, at times, we all wish they had succeeded.

Did have a rather nice dinner with President and Mrs Kennedy at Buckingham Palace in June 1961. He was a charming chap. And President Nixon popped over for lunch in February 1969. Now that was a very strange experience. The cheeky sod nicked a candlestick from the bedroom and denied all knowledge when one asked him. One would never have known if he hadn't blurted the truth out to David Frost years later.

Don't ask one about the Bushes. George Bush Snr was nice enough but God help one; one more state visit with his son and one may have started a nuclear war to distract him. One's not a snob, as you know, but one really does draw the line at being addressed as "Grandma". One knows he meant it affectionately, but then they meant the American War of Independence affectionately as well and that still caused us a bit of a sodding headache.

Still, it was nice that Mr Blair managed to make a friend after all those years of annoying everyone he met. We actually didn't tell Mr Bush that Mr Blair had resigned. He didn't seem to notice, though he did comment that he thought Mr Blair had put on some extra weight over the summer. Awkward.

Of course, despite our colourful history, the United Kingdom has always enjoyed a special relationship with the United States of America. One thinks of them as a mother thinks of a teenage boy: with a mixture of pride and exasperation. And there is no denying that the American division of the British Armed Forces has been awfully useful over time, even if they do have a habit of turning up late for wars and then taking the credit.

Every 4th July, famous throughout the world

as American "Renewal of Independence" Day, one makes a point of calling the president of the day and conducting his appraisal personally. On balance, one has thus far decided to renew their independence, although they have been placed on probation until the end of recorded time.

Australia

The Commonwealth of Australia is one's antipodean Kingdom and proof that the sun still never sets on the British Empire.

We found it in the middle of the sea, just floating around and not adding value to the world economy in any way, shape or form, in the late eighteenth century and since then it has gone from strength to strength. It's a wonder no one had inhabited it before the British (if you don't count the natives, that is; and one's colonial ancestors usually didn't).

It is popularly believed that Britain sent convicts to Australia for punishment. This in fact is not true. They were actually sent there for rehabilitation, as William Petty-FitzMaurice, 2nd Earl of Shelburne, who was Prime Minister at the time, believed that all convicts needed was a "bloody good holiday and a bit of sunshine". And so ships full of them were dispatched to the other side of the world to build a new part of the empire and get a bit of a tan whilst they were at it.

And quite frankly, Australia has held a special place in the hearts of the British ever since. It's nice to know that whilst things are a bit serious up here in the northern hemisphere, where we're a bit busy creating value and driving forward the world economy, one has a little outpost down under where everyone is almost pathologically relaxed.

Queen Victoria never managed to visit, partly due to being terribly sea-sick (it was all she could do to get to the Isle of Wight, and although she was convinced it was three-quarters of the way to Australia, she could never face the final few miles) and mainly due to having the world's biggest empire to rule from London, which took up most of her time. Although she was very keen on it and even had the State of Victoria named after her.

One pops over from time to time, of course; mainly when one's British Airways Gold Card is in danger of expiring. The DoE adores the place – so much so that on several occasions we've seriously looked into having it moved a bit closer. Perhaps swapped with France – which would kill two birds with one stone, so to speak. But on balance we always think it is rather nice down there where it is.

The people of Australia are famously staunchly monarchist of course; aside from a few unstable people who think Julia Gillard would make a better head of state. And they come out in their hundreds of thousands to welcome one whenever one is down under.

It's no coincidence that William and Catherine chose Australia for the first official visit by

Prince George. May as well get the little fellow used to it; we've decided to make him Governor General on his fifth birthday, by which time he'll be the most emotionally developed Governor General they've had down there for approximately 100 years.

They seemed to enjoy it. Catherine texted to say they'd been to a BBQ and that the Australians seem to be managing to cook a shrimp without the help of a Pippa Middleton cookbook. Well there's a surprise.

Have been seriously considering retiring to Australia, actually. Nice little palace by the beach, perhaps. Might get a few convicts out there working on foundations just in case. The sun will do them the world of good.

France

One is technically still Queen of France but we play it down for obvious reasons. It's ironic that our close European neighbour has also been our sworn enemy for most of the last thousand years, yet on the two occasions they've got themselves into hot water with the Germans, we've had to pop over and rescue them after they surrendered.

Still, keeping them in their place is a key strategic aim of the United Kingdom, and to this day all Presidents of France have the word "Agincourt" tattooed onto their left buttock as a reminder of who's in charge.

Although in recent years we have been getting along much better and have even signed a defence treaty whereby we are testing nuclear weapons together. This caused much surprise at the time but it's really not that unusual: the English have been testing nuclear weapons in France for hundreds of years.

Yet there is one victory that escaped the British until 2012: The Tour de France. Despite the British command of the bicycle in recent years, this race had eluded one. Until, in the London Olympic Year, Bradley Wiggins stepped up to the mark and did his bit for Queen and country.

One can remember the day well. François Hollande called in the morning to say he'd arrived safely back in Paris. He'd apparently got the wrong end of the stick when he heard that the British were riding triumphantly into the capital and fled to Switzerland. They've always been a bit nervous since the end of the Hundred Years War. One called Bradley Wiggins and congratulated him on his win and wished him luck for the London Olympics.

At the time, one had been planning on putting up the Olympic rings at Buckingham Palace to get the nation into the Olympic Spirit but Lord Coe called to say that wasn't allowed, as one had not secured the necessary sponsorship rights. He said one could project a giant Big Mac onto Windsor Castle though. Told him to jog on. They seemed to have finally got security sorted though. Apparently Paul McCartney is playing and they're confident that will keep even the most hardened criminal away.

There is of course one thing that the French love more than anything else: a revolution. They literally cannot get enough. They proclaimed a republic in September 1792 and King Louis XVI was executed the next year. Unfortunately for them, King George III had won France in a poker game the previous year and so the whole guillotine thing was a bit of a waste of time, but we didn't have the heart to mention it. Just as well really, since aside from popping over and rescuing them from the Germans occasionally, these days one really tries to limit one's French responsibilities to the occasional booze cruise.

Scottish Holidays

Every summer the Court officially gets on a plane and decamps to Scotland for one's annual highland holiday. One has a little holiday home up there – Balmoral Castle – in Royal Deeside, Aberdeenshire. It's near the village of Crathie, east of Braemar, where they hold the Highland Games.

Prince Albert bought Balmoral as a present for Queen Victoria in 1852, along with a small garden of about 49,000 acres, including grouse moors, forestry and farmland, as well as a few thousand deer, Highland cattle, and ponies. It's a nice little place and makes a change from the big estates one is used to in the south.

The highlight of the holiday is the Highland Games in Braemar. The Scots can put a stone and throw a hammer like nobody's business. It's a shame Lord Coe didn't manage to get them into the Olympic Games but it was generally felt that there were very few countries outside Scotland brave enough to enter.

The DoE is usually on fine form. He's something of an expert in Highland Dancing and can often be seen in his kilt jigging around Balmoral Castle. Mr Cameron and Mr Clegg were unable to join us last year (partly due to not being invited and partly because the Tug of War brings back bad memories of the coalition negotiations for them), although Mr Cameron called to say he would be holding his own sack race in Westminster this week, in the form of a cabinet reshuffle.

The DoE and I often leave slightly before the end to miss the traffic, although Prince Edward stays on.

After a day at the games, it's back to Balmoral for the traditional summer BBQ. One says "summer", but being Scotland that really means that temperatures are not sub-zero between the hours of midday and 1pm, so it's hardly balmy. Although that doesn't stop Prince Harry indulging his nudist tendencies. He does love warming a sausage by the fire.

The DoE has had the Land Rover converted to a moving BBQ, complete with drinks cabinet. It is an ingenious design actually, including a direct feed from the petrol tank to the coal in order to get the fire going before he sticks on a burger.

The tradition of Scottish summers for monarchs was really brought about to temper feeling in Scotland that the union was run a by distant and remote English elite and it was generally thought that the locals would like to see their undoubted imperial leaders once in a while. These days it's used more to check on Alex Salmond and ensure that he's not doing more damage up here than is strictly necessary.

Strangely, if Scotland votes for independence, one's Scottish holidays will officially be state visits, albeit a little more relaxed. Not that it looks very likely. Mr Salmond is actually a huge unionist, although he does have trouble expressing himself. Poor chap has been distraught since he lost a game of Cluedo with Mr Cameron and ended up having to fight an independence referendum.

Still, if they do vote for it it'll be a change in name only, rather like America. We don't actually let these people govern themselves. There's no telling what they might do.

Europeans

Europe is like a geographical version of eBay, with all the major countries continually buying and selling the smaller nations. This system generally works well, although in April 2013 one leased back Cyprus by mistake.

One can remember it well. It was Papal Inauguration Day. Pope Francis called first thing to say how excited he was, although wished he hadn't overdone it on the holy water last night at the traditional karaoke with the cardinals (it's a kind of stag party for popes – one didn't like to ask for all the details).

He said he'd had Cyprus on the phone and had said a few prayers for their economy as requested but they didn't seem to be doing much good so far. One told him to be patient; it was a good couple of years after ascending to the role of Supreme Governor of the Church of England before one started working miracles.

Had no sooner finished off a light breakfast of bacon, eggs, black pudding and fried bread when President Anastasiades of Cyprus texted to ask if one fancied buying the country back ("good price, good price, guarantee", apparently).

One had sold it in 1960 to the Russians, although no one mentioned that to the Greeks and the Turks who have been arguing over it ever since.

Say what you like about British administration, but the whole place really has gone downhill since we moved out. The DoE says it's essentially been transformed into some kind of "Costa Del Essex": Pizza Hut with a sea view and a temperate climate.

Prince Harry said he'd had some memorable nights out in Larnaca but one wasn't entirely sure if that were a good thing or not. They're presumably quite relaxed about nudity though, so that's saying something at least.

Was actually quite relaxed about popping them into the "Euro" file when William Hague called to remind one that we'd kept a couple of "Sovereign Bases" over there. Initially enquired as to what sovereign exactly was based there, as this one has no recollection of a Cypriot holiday home, but apparently they are military bases – something like tropical aircraft hangers, as far as one could tell. Hague was worried that our lads out there might run out of cash so one had an RAF plane filled up with one million Euros and sent over there pronto.

Unfortunately President Anastasiades got the wrong end of the stick and texted to say he was pleased we'd taken the place off his hands and that he'd send back the change on the next boat. Awkward. Still, might make Nick Clegg Governor General or something.

5

Events, Occasions and
Other Things

The Coronation

Despite ascending the Throne is 1952, it wasn't until 1953 that one was crowned. Winston Churchill insisted that we give it some time between one's accession and coronation, mainly so the country could save up a bit of cash and partly because we wanted Prince Charles to be old enough to understand what was going on. We failed on the latter point, sixty years on and he still doesn't have much of a clue where he is.

It's a funny old thing, a coronation, since in this country one has all the power of the sovereign from the moment one's mother or father passes away. Yet one has always felt there's something of significance in being crowned. It's like knowing what you're going to get for Christmas but still finding it exciting opening it.

Of course the main worry beforehand was that it might piss with rain, and whilst the British are accustomed to picnics in sub-zero temperatures, we could really do without having to wring out our cucumber sandwiches. In the event, it was overcast but mainly dry and the RAF even managed a fly past down the Mall before heading on to France to drop some ceremonial bombs and remind the continent who's in charge.

There were 8,000 guests in the Abbey, although quite honestly one didn't know them all personally. One was convinced most of them were there at the coronation of Queen Victoria; the DoE said that one singlehandedly lowered the average age by about 25 years when one walked in.

One was handed the six symbols of authority – the orb, the sceptre, the rod of mercy, the royal ring of sapphire and rubies, the key to the royal gin cupboard and Hitler's left testicle – and the

Archbishop of Canterbury, Dr Geoffrey Fisher, popped St Edward's Crown on one's head to complete the ceremony.

Charles was simultaneously crowned with a party hat so he didn't feel left out, and to this day he still wears it in the bath.

A shout of "God Save the Queen" was heard and gun salutes were fired as crowds cheered.

The whole thing used then to be repeated in India, but sadly one just missed out on the whole Empress of India thing when one's father, King George VI, famously declared "sod them, they can bloody sort it out themselves".

One was crowned Queen of Australia of course, amongst many other nations, and we had momentarily thought about popping over there and restaging the whole thing, but it was generally considered that the Australians don't really go in for formal occasions in that way and one wasn't keen on a beach BBQ and being presented with some kind of ceremonial "shrimp" as an alternative.

It doesn't seem like sixty years. Yet so much has changed. One made a solemn oath to serve one's people one's entire life, be it long or short, and one remains committed to your service. Much to the disappointment of Prince Charles, who is becoming convinced that was the only coronation he'll ever get to attend.

The Diamond Jubilee

The Derby, 1,000 boats on the Thames, a
Gary Barlow organised concert and a carriage
procession through London. It all sounds very
nice but quite frankly one had been hoping for a
rather different Diamond Jubilee celebration.

Starting to wonder if it was a good idea to let
Gary Barlow organise the concert, to be honest.
He was hanging around the Palace with his little
clipboard like some kind of cross between a pop
star and a food hygiene inspector. One thought
for a while that he had actually moved in!

The DoE says he's like a corgi although not as
well trained. And Cliff Richard? Cliff sodding
Richard? What part of "Led Zeppelin" did he not
understand? Still, Elton John was there. Does
he do anything other than Royal births, deaths,

marriages and jubilees these days? He was insisting on doing another version of "Candle in the Wind" ("Hello England's Queen, though we don't know you at all, you have the grace to reign over us, whilst those around you fall" etc. etc.). One told him not to bother.

Although one was looking forward to leading a flotilla up the Thames. One ordered a new barge for the occasion, although the first incarnation was more like a tug than a Royal Barge. One had Zippy and Bungle (Mr Cameron and Boris Johnson) on the phone to talk them through the amount of gold and red that was needed to transport a Queen. This is the United Kingdom after all, not some European Banana republic.

There was a time, of course, when Royal jubilees were celebrated by sinking the entire Spanish Fleet, but it's generally considered rude these days so one makes do with sinking a few European banks instead.

The Derby was the highlight of one's Diamond Jubilee weekend. One could feel a big win coming on. Called the Governor of the Bank of England first thing in case one needed some quantitative easing. Put the Irish economy on the first race; "start small", as the DoE always says.

Thankfully the Middletons didn't tag along again. Mrs "I really would like you to call me Carole" Middleton turned up at Ascot last year in a hat the size of a small colony. Even Princess Beatrice was embarrassed, and that's saying something. They're very pleasant but insist on placing £2.50 each way bets, which quite frankly is awkward. One's poor bookmaker doesn't know if he's coming or going.

Made a quick list of what one might spend the winnings on: 1) new helicopter for William 2) Pippa Middleton for Harry 3) Monaco for the DoE 4) water-pistol for Mr Clegg 5) New Culture Secretary for Mr Cameron 6) English as a foreign language CD for Mr Miliband.

The Diamond Jubilee booze cruise was less of a
success. The DoE started the day off by knocking
up a light breakfast of bacon, eggs, sausages,
potatoes, tomatoes, black pudding, mushrooms,
baked beans and fried bread to get us all off to
a good start. Edward was almost beside himself
with excitement; he loves getting dressed up as a
sailor.

Mr Clegg called first thing to ask if one would
be requiring his inflatable dinghy. He'd got a new
Popeye costume apparently and said he'd be a
very good Deputy Pageant Master. One thanked
him for the offer but said he could spend the
day on the Downing Street Pond where Mr
Cameron is having his own little pageant.

Jumped in the Bentley and headed down to the
Thames about 2ish. Charles and Camilla got
there early, having popped into a street party for
a gin and tonic on the way. No sooner had we
got onto the barge than Camilla was downstairs
looking for duty free.

Watched the rowing boats float past before joining the pageant on the Royal Barge. Camilla had a go at steering for a while and nearly wiped out an entire company of sea cadets and several rowing boats in the process. The DoE stationed himself upfront to look out for icebergs and one settled down to watch the boats. Caught a glimpse of Bungle (Boris Johnson) waving furiously from a passing river taxi and wondered for a minute if the Royal Barge was equipped with artillery.

Just got past Parliament and it started pissing with rain. It really is hard to defend the faith in that weather. Camilla lightened the mood with a spontaneous performance of "rock the boat, don't rock the boat baby, rock the boat, don't tip the boat over" before disappearing below deck to light the end of a crafty cigarette. It was a bit obvious where she'd gone when a huge cloud of smoke emerged, but William said people would probably think the barge was steam powered.

By the time we got to Tower Bridge it was
absolutely sodding freezing. Luckily Catherine
had knitted everyone their own throw, which kept
the worst of the wind off but the DoE said her
nipples could still cut glass. Tower Bridge opened
as we passed (Camilla said it was probably to let
Charles' ego through) and we moored near HMS
Belfast to watch the remaining boats pass.

After about half an hour one was wondering
if we really needed 1,000 boats. It was never
ending. And one's arse was like a block of
sodding ice by the time the Royal Philharmonic
passed and signalled the end of the flotilla. We
had been planning on sailing on to the continent
and firing a few warning shots at the Europeans
but had to abandon the plan due to adverse
weather. The DoE said it was just as well; it
brings back bad memories for the Spanish to
see the British on the water and one didn't like
to rub it in that as one sailed gloriously down
the Thames, the Europeans were drifting up the
proverbial creek without a paddle.

Of course one was very sad that the DoE couldn't join one for the last two days. Poor chap got absolutely sodding soaked at the river parade and said he really couldn't handle watching Cheryl Cole screeching her way through a song at the following evening's concert. One had insisted that all performances were given live but after about thirty seconds one was texting Gary Barlow to tell him one took it all back and commanding him to shut off her microphone. It was like a whistler firework had gone off early.

Thank goodness for Tom Jones – it wasn't until he'd performed that one ventured outside to see it in person. It all went rather well until a bunch of absolute morons scaled the palace and started dancing on the roof. Charles said it was Madness. One couldn't have agreed more. Just as well the DoE wasn't there, he'd have shot them.

Paul McCartney finished up with 'Live and Let Die' (which stuck one as deeply inappropriate) and one lit the final jubilee beacon, followed by Camilla who in turn used it to light a ceremonial cigarette. Not that Gary Barlow is getting a knighthood; any good work in organising the concert has been undone by hanging around at the Palace like a Duchess of York.

On the last day of one's official diamond jubilee celebrations one trotted off to St Paul's for a service of thanksgiving (which doubled as a request for more sunshine). Dumbledore (the Archbishop of Canterbury) was hosting. The Chuckle Brothers (Mr Cameron and Mr Clegg) were there; although one had them seated so far back they were practically in Surrey.

Had lunch at Westminster Hall, via a quick gin-stop at Mansion House, and then back to the Palace in carriages. One has to be seen to be believed. And if there's one thing the British do very well it's a horse-drawn carriage procession. It's such a shame the DoE missed it. He says he's spent more time looking at a horse's arse over the last sixty years than anything else.

Charles and Camilla tagged along as one had a spare seat, which was just as well really as Camilla had bought along a hip-flask of gin. Inside for cheese straws and mini cheddars and then out onto the balcony for the obligatory wave.

One never tires of seeing millions of people surging towards the palace. Of course, in most Middle Eastern countries such a sight would be cause for alarm, but here in London it's treated with pride and excitement. The RAF staged a fly past before heading on to the continent to fire a few warning shots at Merkel and co.

One was so delighted that one addressed the nation to convey one's thanks. We all crowded around the TV to watch it. Charles had recorded his own address to the nation and brought it round on DVD. We put it on and pretended it was being broadcast.

It did all go rather quickly and one was back to work before one knew it. The Flower Pot Men (Mr Cameron and Mr Clegg) came over to bring one down to reality and to update one on their non-progress. Mr Clegg doesn't actually come in for the conversation but we usually give him a cup of orange squash and some Lego to play with whilst he's waiting and he seems quite content.

Sixty years on the throne. Who would have thought it? It was Queen Victoria who first marked a Diamond Jubilee, although she wasn't too bothered about celebrating it.

She didn't even get out of her carriage to attend a Service of Thanksgiving at St Paul's Cathedral. They said at the time this was because she wanted to be amongst her people, and later commentators have surmised that it was due to her failing health, but the truth (as revealed in her secret diaries at Windsor Castle) is that the door of the carriage was a bit stiff and had seized up on route, so she didn't have much choice. Still, she had a seat warmer and a bottle of whisky so was apparently quite happy.

One's own Diamond Jubilee had been in the planning for many, many years. In the event, the London Olympics clashed a bit though. (Mr Blair quite charmingly commented that he hadn't expected one to "make it that far" when bidding for them. One replied that one was quite confident of being in charge long after he'd found himself out on his arse.)

One was quite clear that one wanted it to be a peoples' jubilee, although one hadn't fully appreciated that would involve having a child design one's official Diamond Jubilee logo via a *Blue Peter* competition. All things democratic may be held together with sticky-back plastic and paper, but Royal occasions are usually a bit more solid. Still, not to worry, one went with it. And Edward is never out of his official t-shirt, it has to be said.

Still Reigning

Next jubilee is one's Platinum Jubilee in 2022.
And after one's diamond celebrations one
does rather hope that one is around to see it.
Thousands of beacons lit around the world,
a river pageant, a concert (of sorts) and a
procession through the streets. Made one proud
to be British.

Royal Birthday Parties

Members of the Royal Family have Birthdays in the summer, regardless of when they are actually born. This is so we can have a summer family BBQ to mark the occasion. We jump in ceremonial carriages and ride over to the far end of the Buckingham Palace garden. The DoE's in charge of the BBQ and always gets the fire roaring, although one does wish he wouldn't insist on lighting it with petrol.

One remembers the first time that Catherine had been able to join us. She's an incessant knitter and had turned up with a union flag picnic blanket the size of a small country. Unfortunately she had brought the out-laws with her. Mrs "please call me Carole" Middleton insists on dropping to her knees with a breathless "Your Majesty" every time she sees one. The DoE calls her "Queen-Mother-in-Waiting". Mr Middleton brought a box of Asda value meat and a case of Fosters with him, which quite frankly was more than a little awkward.

We weren't entirely sure what happened to Camilla. She was last seen climbing a tree with a steak knife between her teeth saying she was off to catch squirrels. She has a habit of getting lost and we usually wait until she lights up and follow the smoke signals.

Andrew always attends these things in full Navy uniform. The DoE calls him the Rear Admiral. He's got a little inflatable boat on the Buckingham Palace lake. He's been trying to get back to the Falklands for years; no one's mentioned that the lake is landlocked. Still, keeps him busy and we throw him a sausage about once every half hour when he floats past. Bit of a drama that year though, when he got a slow puncture and William had to rescue him with his helicopter. We were going to throw him a bit of rope but William likes to do these things properly.

Of course, it's one's Birthdays that provide the most excitement in the Royal Household. One does like Birthdays. It's such a shame one only has two each year. There is a real Birthday in April, with an official Birthday to follow in June.

The DoE usually wakes one up with a piece of toast in the shape of a heart and a cup of tea and Edward comes in with one's cards and presents and sits on one's bed whilst one opens them all. It does take a while to get through about 48,507 cards but thankfully we've enough mantelpieces to put them on.

Mr Clegg's card is usually late. He calls about mid-morning to apologise for not having sent it sooner but says he is just finishing off the colouring in and the glitter and he'll pop it round on his bicycle, which is nice.

More than 88 years. More than 60 of them as your undoubted sovereign lady. One wasn't born to be Queen, of course. As one's father, King George VI used to say, "If Edward VIII hadn't swung his leg across that God-awful American woman, Wallis Simpson, we'd have a smaller house but a lot more bloody time on our hands!"

Still, duty calls.

Whilst one has been Queen, one has seen 12 prime ministers, six Archbishops of Canterbury and six Popes; answered about 3.5 million letters (3.4 of which weren't particularly interesting, to be perfectly honest); undertaken 261 official overseas visits to 116 countries (we haven't been to Greece, not since they went all strange and kicked the DoE out); undertaken 30,000 official engagements; and consumed 7,176.5 bottles of gin.

Of course, one has been blessed to have spent much of the past years with the DoE at one's side. What would we do without him?

It hasn't all been easy. As monarch, one has seen some very difficult, unpleasant and demanding times; such as 35 Royal Variety Shows and several performances by Paul McCartney and Elton sodding John (who has a song that can be adapted for every occasion, so it would seem). It's a cross one has to bear.

As one nears the end of one's ninth decade, you may rest assured that one has no intention of slowing down. Your ever loving Queen will not leave you alone with Prince Charles and David Cameron. There's no telling the damage they might do.

The Pope

Something of a love/hate relationship with the Catholic Church. Henry VIII wasn't a fan and set up his own Church in competition. Charles tried to do the same thing in later years, but the idea never really got off the ground (although apparently Tom Cruise was interested).

Over the years, heads of the Church of England and Catholic Church have tended to avoid each other, but when Joey Ratzinger took over as Benedict XVI, he was desperate to "hook up and shoot the shit" (whatever that means).

For years one always managed to find an excuse. Still, we world religious leaders have to show unity these days and so one finally agreed to let him come over in 2010.

Decided to receive him in Scotland – they've always been a bit keener on the whole Catholic thing than the English. He called to say how much he was looking forward to coming over and would one mind if he brought a few cardinals over with him – doesn't like travelling alone, apparently.

No one looked forward to the Papal visit more that the DoE. He says it's amazing that a man who used to be an after dinner mint has come so far. One had to overrule his plan to greet His Holiness dressed as a pregnant nun, although there was no denying that the look on his face would be worth it.

On the day of the visit, the Pope texted first thing to say how excited he was. Did wonder about cancelling for a minute but one's had the drawing room hoovered especially and it seemed a shame to waste it. There was much speculation in the press that one may be sharing the popemobile for this trip. One's press secretary sent a memo to remind them that this Head of State and World Religious leader has a Bentley.

The DoE went to collect him from the airport, thankfully not dressed as a nun, whilst one had a quick brunch libation and some eggs benedict to get in the mood.

They took an age to drive from the airport. Traffic must have been bad. Met him outside, smiled and nodded and whisked him inside for a cup of earl grey and a custard cream. He said the flight had been good, but the food had been bad: he wasn't entirely sure what was in the little tin foil dish but it had apparently played havoc with his constitution. One could relate, having had a very similar experience with Tony Blair.

We soon caught up on the 500 years we haven't been speaking and one took him on a quick tour of the Royal archives to show him how well we've managed without Papal leadership. Gave him a few custard creams in some cling film for the journey, popped him in his little glass box popemobile thing and waved him off. (The DoE thought if the popemobile was red it would look just like Postman Pat's van.)

It was after that meeting that the incessant texting started: "where did you get your hat/ Bentley/palace/husband/who is Nick Clegg?" etc. One didn't reply: one doesn't like to encourage too regular contact. He seemed pleased with his visit though. Felt that he'd "finally regained the moral upper hand from Bono".

Relations have been cordial ever since. If there's one thing one's good at, it's building bridges. The DoE thinks one should have been a structural engineer. We haven't seen each other since, but he often texts, especially during key world events, such as the Eurovision Song Contest and Led Zeppelin reunion concerts.

One suspects he would like to meet regularly, but one does have to remind him that "the Bishop of Rome hath no jurisdiction in this Realm of England", especially ex-Bishops.

Still, Pope Francis seems promising. One popped over in April 2014 to officially anoint him, bring him up to speed on the more progressive Church of England, discuss excommunicating Tony Blair, sainthood for Freddie Mercury etc.

He said after only a few months in the job he felt he was finally finding his feet, and that the bright red slippers helped.

The President of Argentina had apparently been hoping he'd use his position to lobby one to give up the Falklands but after a brief (three-hour) synopsis of the last time Rome tried to assert its authority over England, he decided that it probably wasn't worth the bother.

The Pope

One arrived bearing gifts, of course: a little
hamper of goodies from the Royal Farms and
some of Charles' home-baked Duchy Original
biscuits. He said he was thrilled but one could
tell he was feeling a bit awkward that we'd spent
so much. Should have given him something
cheaper. Like Greece.

Honours

Once one has finally recovered from Christmas celebrations at Sandringham, one traditionally gets back to business and hands out a few New Year Honours.

The Olympics dominated after 2012, of course. Unfortunately one can't honour oneself, although one's entrance at the Opening Ceremony was clearly worthy of particular recognition.

Decided to make Bradley Wiggins a Sir for services to sport and cycling, and mainly so the DoE can refer to him as "Knight Rider". Dave Brailsford was also Knighted, Sarah Storey was made a Dame and Grainger, Pendleton, Kenny and Trott were all made CBEs and OBEs for services to public transport, having encouraged a nation to give up on the tube and get on their bikes.

In British maritime tradition, Ben Ainslie was Knighted for services to sailing. We may have slipped a bit since seeing off the Spanish Armada but Britannia still rules the waves.

Jessica Ennis and Mo Farah were made CBEs for services to sport and athletics and Andy Murray has been awarded an MBE for services to acting following his emotional interview after losing the Wimbledon final. This was upgraded to OBE when he finally won the bloody thing – although will be downgraded to a sticker if Scotland votes for independence.

Away from sport, one made Cherie Blair a CBE for putting up with Mr Blair for all these years. Funnily enough she's quite happy to accept an honour from her Queen even if she makes a point of not curtseying to her. Strange how all these raging republicans are quite happy to be associated with royalty when it's in their self-interest.

Also made Tracey Emin a CBE as a thank you for the artwork she gave one for one's Diamond Jubilee, which incidentally has made one a tidy little profit on eBay.

Lord Coe was made a Companion of Honour on the strict understanding he will never, ever, give a public speech again, and the Met police Commissioner Bernard Hogan Howe was knighted for services to Downing Street policemen.

Politicians, of course, are never forgotten, and some years one recognises the entire Cabinet in the New Year Dishonours for services to economic decline. Mr Clegg was additionally made a Pantomime Dame for his grovelling apology for making the tuition fees U-turn. Margaret Beckett was made a Dame for being in politics for longer than anyone can remember whilst achieving absolutely nothing of note.

A special mention went to Stella McCartney who was awarded an OBE for services to fashion from such humble beginnings. How difficult it must be to start a business with a multi-millionaire and world famous father.

The Eurovision Song Contest

One loves Eurovision day. It serves as an annual reminder of just how strange things are over there on the continent. Last year, we had the family over for a pre-Eurovision BBQ at Windsor Castle first. The Middletons came over with several packs of Morrisons value ribs and a case of Heineken, which was quite frankly awkward in the extreme. And who knew Mrs "if you can't call me Carole on Eurovision night, when can you" Middleton drank neat Pimms? Still, a nice afternoon was had by all.

Every year one holds a Royal Eurovision Fancy Dress party in the evening. Princesses Beatrice and Eugenie came last year as Jedward, which for Beatrice meant toning down the hat for once. The DoE came as Engelbert Humperdinck and did a quick if slightly drunk version of 'Please

Release Me' to get us all in the mood. William, Catherine, Harry and Pippa Middleton were a very convincing ABBA. Sadly Camilla misread the invitation as "Euro-Crisis Fancy Dress" and came as Greece. Awkward.

Engelbert was up first that year. Poor chap pulled the short straw in Gary Barlow's "Queen's Jubilee Concert or Eurovision" raffle. Gave it a good shot, although the Queen of Spain texted half way through saying "hahahahaha!". One didn't reply. Mr and Mrs Clegg provided the backing dancing. He likes to help out, bless him.

Things are clearly worse than one thought in Eastern Europe. All Russia could manage was six grannies, with only five teeth between them as far as one could tell. It was like the "Six Wives of Lenin". President Putin called to assure one it had absolutely nothing to do with him but the DoE's convinced they're his personal bodyguard.

There were a few power ballads about collapse of the Euro, illegitimacy of the European Court and that kind of thing, which must have felt very difficult in Brussels. Greece did their best to show the world what happens in a country with no money and no government. The place hasn't been the same since the DoE left, to be honest.

Jedward provided the Irish entry, proving that Ireland has adopted the Euro in more ways than one. You've got to feel sorry for them. The irony of twins who can't sing in time isn't lost on your Queen. By the time they'd finished one was seriously considering putting Ireland on eBay.

The DoE spent a fair percentage of the Civil List voting for Greece, although only to see the look on the faces of European Central Bankers if they won. But alas victory for Sweden. As if King Carl XVI Gustaf isn't cocky enough.

Seriously thinking of adopting the Eurovision format to decide upon future entries/exits from the Eurozone. Mr Cameron's very keen on the idea. He says that it's probably the surest and least painful way to get Britain out.

The Eurovision Song Contest – the French call it "Concours Eurovision de la Chanson", which frankly sounds a bit pretentious – has its origins in the aftermath of World War II. The original format was that heads of Government would enter on behalf of their countries. It's a little known fact that Hitler was a terrible singer and an atrocious dancer (although, to be fair, they weren't his worse qualities) and it was widely believed that had the German people known this they would never have elected him.

It's become something of a political litmus test in recent times: Jedward representing Irish economic humiliation, for example, and the slow withdrawal of the British from "giving a shit" as the DoE would say. There's a silver lining around Britain's failure to win for a generation and that is we don't have to host the bloody thing over here. There is only one thing worse than Europeans on the streets of England and that's singing Europeans.

The London Olympics

The London Olympics were seven years in the planning. Seb Coe had virtually moved into the Palace and one was glad to see the back of him, to be honest. The DoE took to asking him to demonstrate the 1,500 metres just to get rid of him.

It didn't look as if it were going to be a success at the start though. One remembers the "G4S weekend". One had an epic hangover. The Duchess of Cornwall and I spent most of the weekend stranded on a cheese island in the middle of a sea of gin. Uneasy laid the head that wore a crown that morning, that's for sure. Still, nothing that a light breakfast of bacon, eggs, black pudding, fried potatoes, tomatoes, mushrooms and baked beans didn't sort out.

The Home Secretary called first thing to ask if one "had any spare soldiers hanging around to help with Olympic security". Apparently G4S have had a "minor recruitment" problem leaving a little gap of about 3,500 staff. One asked if seven years hadn't been enough notice for a little recruitment drive, especially considering that there are one or two people out of work, but the Home Secretary said it was all down to problems created by the last Government, the Euro crisis, the drought and the flooding etc., and that there was nothing more that could have been done.

The DoE suggested sending a few corgis round to help out but it was thought that might not be the best idea, what with their inbred intolerance of politicians and everything. Monty the corgi has developed quite a dislike of Mr Cameron in particular, expressed by way of the rather awkward habit of biting him in the arse whenever he bends over, which makes bowing quite a traumatic experience for the poor chap. He smiles and says it's not a problem but the DoE thinks he must have a very bruised coalition.

Just as well one's armed forces were available at such short notice to fill the gap. Can't help but wonder if cutting 20,000 soldiers seemed like such a good idea just at that moment but Mr Cameron assured one it was all under control. Well that's all right then.

Anyway, after a shaky start, it all went rather well.

Had about 95 heads of state and government over for gin cocktails and cheese straws at the Palace before it all kicked off as a welcome to Britain. The Queen of Spain managed to make it after all (the Germans gave her a lift, apparently), which was nice. She said she was not overly fussed about the Olympics but very excited about the possibility of meeting Phillip Schofield (she loves that man). Kim Jong Un couldn't make it, which is just as well as we don't have a North Korean flag, and Mitt Romney was due to attend but had to cancel at the last moment (coincidentally at the same time as one had him deported).

James Bond popped over to the Palace to pick one up for the opening ceremony in a helicopter. One had been planning on taking the Bentley but, with London at a virtual standstill, one thought one might not arrive until the closing. Of course, a trick of the camera made it look like one had parachuted into the stadium, when in fact one simply abseiled.

One had to hand it to Danny Boyle, the main event was very impressive. There was a touching moment when Mr Clegg sang with the rest of his school choir and an awkward moment when Rowan Atkinson did a part as Mr Bean and the President of the International Olympic Committee said he thought Ed Miliband was looking well. The DoE thought the highlight of the night was the NHS scene, although the part where David Cameron comes on and ceremoniously sacks the nurses was cut due to shortage of time.

Not entirely sure what the French commentary was all about. One texted Danny Boyle and pointed out that we are on the right side of the channel over here and that seemed to sort it. Angela Merkel called to say how happy she was that this wasn't taking place anywhere else in Europe (presumably because she'd be paying for it).

The usual parade of athletes served to remind us all that there are, strictly speaking, far too many countries in the world. The DoE and I played "spot the ones we own", which is like a kind of colonial bingo, to pass the time. Surely that's more countries than we actually need. Are all of them real? Popped a few, that looked like they could do with parliamentary democracy, railways and roads etc., on one's shopping list for future reference.

The DoE had bought Lord Coe a *Dummies Guide to World Flags*, so all seemed to go without a hitch. The Commonwealth flags are the best, let's be honest. Had seriously considered giving the USA the Union Flag to parade under but it was generally felt they wouldn't appreciate the joke.

After what seemed like a lifetime of flags and a speech by Lord Coe, which was at least twice as long as he was strictly allocated, one kept one's speech short and sweet (much like oneself) and did the necessary opening. The world was once again reminded that the Olympic anthem is far too long before the symbolic lighting of the cauldron.

The flame arrived by speedboat, courtesy of David Beckham's new river taxi business. One wasn't sure what else to do with him, to be honest; clearly a speech was out of the question. The cauldron was lit by the next generation of British athletes and Camilla threw a fag end into

a special box to start the fireworks before Mr
Bean ended the show with a Paul McCartney
impression.

Headed back to the palace for an Olympic sized
gin and tonic with no tonic and retired safe in
the knowledge that nobody does it better than
the British.

Years of defending the faith had finally paid
off with some sunshine at long last. One
was starting to wonder if a summer palace
somewhere tropical might have been in order.
Emergency conference call with the Pope at
the weekend seemed to have done the trick; we
agreed to petition the Almighty in the name of
the Catholic and Anglican Churches.

Mr Clegg was over the moon. He had his
paddling pool out in the Downing Street garden
for the first time that summer. Mr Cameron's
apparently keeping him covered in "Factor 50"
sunscreen to stop him getting burned, but you

just can't keep him out of the water when it's sunny.

By day four TeamGB were in fighting spirit. One had just about recovered from the Opening Ceremony. The International Olympic Committee called to confirm that one won gold in the parachuting/abseiling, which as it would turn out was the first that week for TeamGB.

Camilla was a bit upset that 007 hadn't accompanied her to the Opening Ceremony but said she was looking into securing Phillip Schofield for future appearances. Never one to be outdone, Charles had apparently taken to abseiling into rooms when on official business, which caused some confusion at Buckingham Palace one morning when the DoE nearly shot him thinking he was an intruder.

Prince Harry called to say he'd seen TeamGB win bronze in the men's gymnastics. They'd apparently originally been in line for Silver but

the Japanese protested (they're prone to that sort
of thing over there) and had it downgraded to
Bronze. Made a few phone calls to enquire about
having Japan's credit rating downgraded to
Bronze as well and made a mental note to bring
it up next time one has the Emperor over for a
pizza.

Princess Anne, William, Catherine and
Harry were out in force to cheer on the Show
Jumping in the final stages of the Eventing this
afternoon. Zara was competing on her horse
High Kingdom (named after Great Britain,
obviously). Good show all round, although Zara
didn't ride clear – she'd apparently caught sight
of John Major in the audience who has a bizarre
habit of miming "I love you" whenever he sees
a Royal and that distracted her somewhat. Still,
a very well deserved Silver medal. She texted
to say "Bollocks" but one assured her that her
grandmother, Queen and nation were very
proud of them all.

Angela Merkel called in a bit of a panic to check that the German victory hadn't cost her any more money but one assured her that they won't be hosting the Games in Berlin for a good few years yet. She said it wasn't Germany hosting them that was worrying her and that she was just praying that Madrid don't get them anytime soon.

Princess Anne presented the medals and then joined Zara and the rest of the team in a horsebox for the traditional celebratory kebab and ale. She said she'd been warmed by the support the team had received from people up and down the country (Mr Clegg has apparently not moved from his rocking horse all afternoon, he's been so excited).

Called Lord Coe for an update on the ticketing situation. He said one could "rest assured" he was doing all he could to fill the empty seats. One told him he could "rest assured" one would have him de-Lorded if it weren't sorted pronto.

Finished the day in the Olympic spirit
by performing a triple-somersault into a
competition-sized gin and an epic Olympic
celebration with the Duchess of Cornwall. No
idea where she ended up. The last one saw of
her she was getting into a helicopter with Mr
Bond and a Union Flag parachute. Charles
said he'd heard she'd ended up in someone's
fishpond in Staines and went to investigate.
Woke up with a Queen Mother of a hangover,
although nothing that a bacon and black
pudding roll didn't sort.

Just as one thought TeamGB couldn't get any
better, they delivered six gold medals and a silver
– Britain's greatest day in the Olympics for 100
years. One was delighted, not least of all because
one had a bet on with the Queen of Spain that
we'd finish the day with more than twelve gold (so
that's Gibraltar safe for another few years then).
She'd not had a good week, bless her. Only three
medals and not a single gold. And to top it all off,
Phillip Schofield wasn't returning her calls (she

does love that man). Even Kazakhstan got five gold, and they're not even a real nation.

Mrs "it's been more than a year, I do wish you'd call me Carole" Middleton called to say she'd been "glued to the screen". She'd apparently seen a 2000% increase in Union Flag sales from her online party business and said that if Jessica Ennis won gold she'd a good mind to treat herself to a new caravan. Awkward.

Angela Merkel called to say she was relieved that the rest of Europe was outside the top four. She gets a bit confused between the Olympics and the Eurovision Song Contest and she's petrified that the next one will have to be hosted on the continent – which would obviously mean she'd be paying. Didn't look good for Greece either, after one week they were four hundred medals in deficit.

The British football team didn't make it into the medals unfortunately. Although the DoE said it probably came as a relief to them that they wouldn't be required to sing the national anthem again – they do struggle with the words (or any words, come to think of it).

British dominance continued at the cycling. Mr Osborne was over the moon. He became a total cycling convert during that week. Mr Cameron said he was sure he'd be riding without stabilisers before the year is out (he wasn't).

One had planned on dropping into the Olympic Stadium for the athletics one evening but Camilla was still missing with one's parachute. The DoE and I watched it all on the BBC with enough gin to fill an Olympic swimming pool. By the time Jessica Ennis had won the Heptathlon, the DoE's bladder could hardly take the excitement.

A gold in the long jump and before one knew it a gold in the 10,000 metres. Seriously considered ennobling them all, if Mr Clegg doesn't manage to replace the House of Lords with a garden centre, or whatever he's planning.

William hot-footed it over to see the presentations (Seb Coe managed to get in on the act by presenting the flowers). We ended the day third in the medals table with fourteen golds, seven silvers and eight bronze. The Empire Strikes Back.

Well, no sooner had it started than it finished. 29 gold for TeamGB and, with the rest of one's Commonwealth Realms included, one easily topped the medal table. Clearly having a Queen around helps sporting performance, unless you're Spain of course.

One had been due to attend the closing ceremony by parachuting in with a fire extinguisher and putting out the Olympic flame, but Mr Bond was called away on urgent business and took one's helicopter with him. Still, Prince

Harry was happy to take one's ticket and took
Catherine with him. One stayed in with the DoE
and watched it all on TV with an unfeasibly
large gin and a bag of mini cheddars.

Very impressive start to the show. No idea how
they managed to get the London Eye into the
stadium so quickly. It was still on the South
Bank when one drove past that afternoon. The
DoE didn't think that the motorway scene
was realistic though, as the traffic was actually
moving and there were no Olympic lanes. The
humour theme continued when Del Boy and
Rodney (Mr Cameron and Mr Clegg) arrived
dressed as Batman and Robin.

One was surprised to see the morons who scaled
one's roof at the jubilee concert managed to
gatecrash again. Camilla said it was Madness.
The DoE was half way up The Mall with a
shotgun but couldn't get a taxi for love nor
money.

Edward was beside himself with excitement when the Pet Shop Boys came on but it quickly died down when One Direction appeared. They seem like nice enough little girls but after about two minutes of them "singing" there was only one direction that one wanted to see them going in and that was the exit.

Part one finished with a reminder that there are at least 500 too many athletes in the world. Did they really all compete? Really? There was one pretend country in the parade but one was sworn to secrecy so couldn't reveal which one. Once all the athletes were in the stadium they were all arranged in the formation of the Union Flag. The whole world under the British; nearly brought a tear to one's eye.

A few last minute medal presentations and it was on with the music. We got the first few lines of 'Bohemian Rhapsody' before John Lennon took over to remind us all that he was the more talented side of the Beatles partnership.

Jessie J and a bunch of people one had never heard of arrived in a fleet of Royal Rolls Royces. One checked carefully for damage when they returned, one can assure you. It was all going very well until the Spice Girls turned up in taxis. The Sodding Spice Girls. One thought for a moment that Victoria Beckham was about to fall off the roof of one of them – which would have triggered a spontaneous public holiday by way of celebration – but sadly one wasn't that lucky. Prince Harry said he was glad they did a couple of songs as it gave him a chance to "nip out and have a pee".

Freddie Mercury saved the day before Brian May took over for 'We Will Rock You'. Unfortunately Jessie J invaded the stage in one of Freddie Mercury's leotards and did a bit of a karaoke performance, which was awkward, but Brian May seemed to cope with it OK.

The Greek flag was raised to announce the winner of the sovereign debt race before we were given a glimpse of just how bizarre the opening ceremony in Rio will be in four years' time.

Lord Coe and the President of the International Olympic Committee did their best to bring down the mood with about seven hours of speeches before the London Fire Brigade extinguished the flame and The Who closed the show.

People have been asking what happened to Paul McCartney and Elton John. One has three words: Tower of London.

Trooping the Colour

Official Birthday! There are many advantages to being Queen, but having two Birthdays each year is up there with the best of them. Edward comes in first thing and wakes one up by jumping on the bed. He's more excited about one's official Birthday than one is.

Last year one opened the official cards and called Adele and Clare Balding to let them know one had made them MBEs and OBEs respectively. Clare Balding was a bit upset as she'd been expecting a Dame but Adele seemed quite happy, although one wasn't entirely sure she knew what an MBE was. Told her it was kind of like a Brit Award, only internationally recognised.

Made Nick Clegg a Dame for services to humour. That year's Birthday Dishonour went to George Osborne for reasons that should be obvious. Ed Miliband got a Blue Peter Badge for effort, if not achievement.

Got one's Trooping the Colour swag on. Keeping it Royal. It was a bit strange as it was the first year without the DoE but he called to wish one a good time. He said he was relieved not to have to see Mr Cameron, but one knew he was wishing he were there. Still, he's on the mend and that's the main thing. The intravenous gin has made the world of difference, apparently.

Did wonder about taking the Bentley instead of a carriage for a change. Nothing worse than having a draught blowing across one's crown jewels. But after about half an hour of trying we simply couldn't persuade the horses to pull the car so a carriage it was. Took a hard top though for draught reasons.

The Duke of Kent hitched a ride as one had a spare seat. Charles, William and Anne rode alongside and Edward went ahead in an open top carriage in full military uniform, mainly because he likes a hat with a feather.

Catherine was there in her last public engagement before delivering an heir. Mr and Mrs Middleton couldn't make it, unfortunately – mainly due to not being invited. But Mrs "please call me Carole" Middleton called to say she'd be watching it on TV as long as they managed to fix the aerial on the caravan.

One does like military music but it might be nice if they mixed it up a bit every now and then. Note to self, really must put in a few requests next year. One defies any soldier not to enjoy marching to 'We Will Rock You'.

All the usual walking around and turning around and stamping and flag carrying and then back to the Palace for a fly past from the RAF and the usual balcony appearance. This year the RAF are flying on to Europe to pick up Bonnie Tyler, who's refusing to leave until she's won Eurovision, apparently.

Another year, another Official Birthday. Missed the DoE. But couldn't help but think that William and Catherine will be doing this one day. The show must go on.

The Chelsea Flower Show

The Chelsea Flower Show is a bit of a highlight in the Royal calendar. One remembers one's visit in the diamond jubilee year particularly well. One had headed back to Buckingham Palace from Windsor and spent the afternoon weeding the Busy Lizzies before nipping over to the Chelsea Flower Show for a sneak preview before it opened to the masses.

Was greeted by an enormous flowerbed spelling out "The Queen's Diamond Jubilee" in about 30,000 plants. The DoE wondered if it might be rearranged into "Sod the Hosepipe Ban" but apparently there wasn't any time.

What one had originally mistaken for scaffolding overgrown with weeds was in fact a new "24m (80ft) pyramid-shaped garden", complete with a shower. Cliff Richard was at the top singing his heart out but thankfully we couldn't hear him from the ground. There was a bellboy to take one up the levels in a lift, but one politely declined the option of a stainless steel tube to slide back down. When the show is finished it's going to be installed as a fire exit for Downing Street.

Alan Titchmarsh was there, as usual, reigning supreme like the Gary Barlow of the gardening world. The DoE asked him if he was growing any "special weed", which was awkward. One does wish he wouldn't speak to one as if he were an old school-friend. He's as bad as Mrs "honestly, it's been more than a year, please call me Carole" Middleton.

Had a quick whizz round before retiring to the gin-tent for a regal libation before jumping into the Bentley and finishing off a tube of Pringles on the way back to the Palace. Once one pops, one can't stop.

Royal Portraits

What is it about artists that makes them think one wants another sodding portrait of oneself? As if it's not tiresome enough seeing one's face whenever one posts a letter or puts a tenner on a horse, every artist on the planet is queuing up to "interpret" one on canvas.

One wouldn't mind, but if one sees another single portrait of one looking like a Spitting Image puppet, one will end up with some kind of complex.

They do seem popular though. It's a little known fact that Nick Clegg has a sticker book of every portrait of one that has ever been painted.

It's all we've been able to do to persuade Prince Charles to stick to landscapes. He did paint

Camilla once, although that was by mistake. She was standing very still whilst he was decorating the hall at Clarence House and he thought she were a chimney breast, apparently.

The last one was Dan Llywelyn Hall having a crack at revealing one's inner-self in a portrait for the Welsh Rugby Union. Anyone would think that one were playing rugby for Wales, he's made one look so big. We've respectfully requested it hang somewhere with a light footfall (like a store cupboard, for example).

Lucian Freud's attempt wasn't much better, mind you. Always struck one as if he'd finished it and then spilt a glass of water across it and tried to sponge it off. The DoE says he should have stuck to psychoanalysis. It's a wonder he finished it at all after one repeatedly refused to pose in the nude.

One has to hand it to Andy Warhol, though. His portraits of one from 1985 are a particular favourite. In fact, we have one hanging in the downstairs loo at Sandringham. It always cheers one up when one's on the throne.

And Chris Levine managed to capture one in one's happiest state: asleep. It was a holographic portrait, and quite frankly a bit of a wasted opportunity that one wasn't made to be winking at the viewer from different angles. Still, probably just as well – one does like to be selective at whom one winks.

And then of course there's Rolf Harris. One wasn't sure at the time if he were filming a TV series or painting a portrait but he seems to have done a reasonable job of both. Never happy with the finished result though, always felt it needed a bit of touching up.

Now there is one particular artist who always manages to capture one at one's best: the Duke of Edinburgh. Yes, on balance the DoE would definitely be one's favourite.

Royal Ascot and The Derby

Royal Ascot week. Or, as the Keeper of the Privy Purse likes to call it, "transfer-a-sizable percentage-of-the-civil-list-to-one's-bookmaker week".

The DoE gave it a miss last year, on account of recovering from his operation, but the old boy managed to knock up a round of bacon sandwiches for breakfast whilst one dealt with the morning's State Papers (*Racing Post*).

Charles and Camilla kept one company in the carriage whilst the DoE was away, although, whilst Charles knows roughly where to sit on a horse, he's not renowned for his racing skills. Told him the going was firm and he thought one was suggesting he'd need a cushion for the Royal Box.

Called the new Governor of the Bank of England to warn him that one was betting on a scale he's probably not experienced in Canada. He said to call if quantitative easing was required.

Day one doesn't usually end wonderfully, one doesn't mind telling you, although the bookies apparently make a killing on the colour of one's hat (and come to think of it, Camilla does take an unusual interest in what one is wearing before we leave the palace. Shrewd operator, that one). One usually goes for a matching coat. If there's one thing this fashion Queen knows how to do it's colour block.

Finally won the Gold Cup with Estimate (The DoE named him Estimate mainly because his winning would mean we were able finally to look at the estimate for repairing the roof at Buckingham Palace without sending the Treasury into a terminal decline), bringing 200 years of the Ascot Gold Cup without a reigning Sovereign winning to an end!

One's Estimate stormed home for mummy!

Well, that's the mortgage on Ireland paid off. One had been quietly confident actually and stuck a few £million on the nose for good measure. You don't get enough money to buy a continent by betting small, as Queen Victoria used to say. One knew Estimate would do it, mainly because one quietly owned every other horse in the race and had been fattening them up for months.

Andrew was there to present one with the cup. Took a photo of it and texted it to the DoE who was recuperating at Windsor Castle. He said he would fill the swimming pool up with gin so we could celebrate in style when one got back.

Well that's the precedent set, one's betting large from now on. At this rate one'll be able to pay off that enormous bill Mr Clegg ran up on games when he borrowed Mr Cameron's iPhone.

Of course the big hope at Ascot is that Princess Beatrice doesn't make an appearance, to be honest. The last thing we need is one of her hats startling the horses.

One traditionally has Mr and Mrs Middleton in the Royal Box on the Thursday. They part-own a horse apparently (the DoE says it's "probably the arse end") so having them over in the Royal Box is the least one could do. One just hopes there isn't a repeat of Derby Day when Mr Middleton asked the Countess of Wessex for a lager and lime, thinking she was a waitress. Awkward.

Mrs "we're all horse owners here, I do wish you'd call me Carole" Middleton likes to place her usual £2.50 each way bets whilst wondering why she isn't winning enough to pay off the mortgage. Although one can relate, quite frankly, having spent the last year trying to pay off the mortgage of Cyprus by way of betting slips alone.

Spotted the chief executive of Tesco on the way out last year, presumably looking for suitable burger material. Mr and Mrs Middleton's horse is looking nervous already.

The DoE scared the life out of one when he appeared in Hosni Mubarak fancy dress, complete with facemask a couple of years ago. One told him there was no way he was wearing that to the Derby, no matter how funny he'd find the look on everyone's faces.

We usually think about taking the open-top Range Rover to Epsom but end up deciding against it, mainly because it is almost always absolutely sodding freezing, and opt for the state Bentley instead. Unfortunately one's driver took a wrong turn last year and we ended up driving to the Royal Box along the racecourse, which was a bit awkward. Still, one smiled and nodded and we seemed to get away with it.

Katherine Jenkins is usually waiting outside the car to sing the national anthem in an extraordinarily small dress. The DoE likes to take one look at her and announce the going is "good to firm". One gives him the benefit of the doubt and assumes he is talking about the racecourse.

Mr and Mrs Middleton are regulars in the Royal Box at Ascot these days, and they do like to arrive early. Mr Middleton says he likes to beat the traffic and leaves home at 2am just to be on the safe side. There is usually an awkward moment when Mr Middleton asks Princess Michael of Kent for a Pimms, thinking she is a waitress.

One usually loses a fortune at the Derby. It starts to feel a bit like Greece in the Royal Box for a while there but one usually makes it up on the third race and texts Johnny English (Mr Miliband) the good news that the deficit won't be getting any bigger after all.

6

Letters from Her Majesty

To Mr Obama on His Application for a Second Term

Dear Mr Obama,

Thank you for your application to be President of America for four more years. Having given the matter some serious thought – and having met the other shortlisted candidate – one is pleased to tell you that you have been successful and that you may remain president until 2016, or until American independence is revoked (whichever is sooner).

The DoE has written to your opponent, Twit Romney, to express our commiserations. (Actually, to be quite honest, he has sent him a text saying "loser", but you get one's meaning.) Do try and go gently with him for a while, the poor chap seems very upset that he won't have the opportunity to start all sorts of wars. One has it on good authority that he'd bought the army face paint and everything.

Mr Cameron (that's the British Prime Minister) has asked one to express his congratulations on your second term and to say how much he is looking forward to working for/with you over the coming years. Mr Clegg (Mr Cameron's work experience intern) has offered to pop over and form a coalition if you find yourself having any trouble with the House of Representatives.

One will be in touch shortly to agree your KPIs and personal development plan for the coming year. However, there are one or two issues that one would like you to give some thought to straight away:

1. "American" English. There really is no such thing as American English. There is The Queen's English and there are mistakes. One should be awfully grateful if you'd

pass that on to computer manufacturers

2. The Eurovision Song Contest. Are you sure you don't fancy taking part? One wouldn't usually ask but one really can't handle another year of European depression expressed via music

3. Would you like Ireland? One can give you a very good price (but you'd have to collect it)

With every good wish
Your undoubted Sovereign Lady
Elizabeth R

To Mrs Merkel on Her Re-election as Chancellor of Greece

Dear Mrs Merkel,

One was delighted to hear that the German people have re-elected you as Chancellor of Greece, Governor of the Bank of Spain and Minister for Debt of Italy. One understands that the celebrations in southern Europe have already started, with people out on the streets starting bonfires and shouting to mark the momentous occasion. They must be thrilled.

It is comforting to know that someone of your experience is holding the wheel in Europe. As one's ancestor the Kaiser used to say, "Look after the Spanish and the Germans will look after themselves."

To Mrs Merkel

You must be disappointed at the prospect of many more years of coalition though. One can relate of course; having at least another 18 months of Daffy Duck and Bugs Bunny (Cameron and Clegg) running the United Kingdom, like two toddlers in a sandpit fighting over the spade.

As your undoubted Sovereign lady and over-lord, one wanted to take this opportunity to set out a few priorities for the coming months of your new term in office.

1. The Eurovision Song Contest. Can we discuss? It's just that one seems to be paying a bloody great big share of the bill without a noticeable amount of success. One wonders if we ought to get Putin on the case to pick up the tab?
2. Isn't it about time you started using a real currency again, rather than Monopoly money? The DoE says a Euro is "not worth a fart in a jar" and one worries

that he has a point. Although don't get any ideas about adopting sterling. We're keeping the real money firmly this side of the Channel.

3. Are you absolutely, entirely sure you don't want Bono? As you know, he was part of the deal when one bought Ireland a number of years ago and one wouldn't mind moving him on, to be quite honest.

4. The King of Spain asked one to ask if he could have his country back?

5. One doesn't like to complain, as you know, but there's a squeaking sound coming from the wheel of one's Bentley and in all likelihood it's not one of the bits that the British built. Could you ask someone your end to take a look?

6. Mr Osborne asked if you fancied buying the lease on Cyprus? We bought it by mistake.

To Mrs Merkel

One wishes you a happy and successful further
four years in office.
Europe owes you a great debt. Literally.
As ever your loving Queen.
Elizabeth R

To Pope Benedict XVI
on His Resignation

Your Holiness,

Thank you for the text message this morning informing one of your resignation. One does apologise for not replying straight away but one had an early morning meeting with a bacon sandwich, which overran.

One was aware that you have been thinking of "going Dutch" and following the example of the Queen of the Netherlands for some time, particularly after you were unsuccessful in your application for the post of Archbishop of Canterbury.

One must say though that one would have

thought you might have waited until after
Valentine's Day to make the announcement.

One will remember with affection your visit to
the United Kingdom in 2010, (the first visit by a
Pope since we went our own religious way), and
catching up on the 500 years we haven't been
speaking.

The people of the United Kingdom will certainly
remember seeing you driving around in your
little Popemobile like a religious Postman
Pat delivering your message first thing in the
morning, when the day is dawning.

Prince Charles of course is very upset. First
Queen Beatrice and now yourself: two world/
religious vacancies that he is sadly not eligible
to apply for. One has explained though that,
whilst standing down before the job is done may
be all the rage on the continent, this side of the
Channel it is considered a little self-indulgent.

One shall look forward to working with your successor. One understands that Tony Blair has already sent off for an application pack. Although one must admit that if there is to be smoke associated with Tony Blair going up a chimney, one sincerely hopes it's not proclaiming him leader of a world religious movement (or any movement, come to think of it).

Needless to say, you have one's very best wishes for a long and happy retirement. One knows that you are looking forward to having more time to yourself, and one does hope that the snowboarding lessons go well.

Keep in touch – one does love to receive your texts.

As ever your loving Queen.
Elizabeth R
Queen, Defender of the Faith, Supreme Governor of the Church of England. Still reigning.

The Queen's message to the People of Romania and Bulgaria

Dear people of Romania and Bulgaria,

As many of you prepare to head for new European shores when your passports finally become valid in countries that you have heard of, you may be considering a trip to one's principal island and home, the United Kingdom.

Please take absolutely no notice of Nigel Farage's attempts to discourage you. As one always says, it is entirely understandable why people would like to flee the continent for one's green and pleasant land.

To help you settle in when you arrive, one has compiled a list of one's top tips for migrating to the United Kingdom:

1. The UK is a wonderful place for swimming. In fact, during the winter months of September to June, swimming is the only way to travel through parts of South West England and almost all of Wales.

2. On arrival, you may be under the impression that the UK is one country. It is in fact five: England, Wales, Scotland, Northern Ireland and Swindon.

3. The UK is a wonderful place for fiction and you may come here expecting to find some familiar places and concepts that in fact do not exist, such as Midsomer and Inspector Barnaby, Coronation Street, the Liberal Democrats and democracy.

4. You'll notice *Ski Sunday* on your TV in January and may wonder what it's all about. It is in fact a documentary about people trying to leave the country when Heathrow and Gatwick airports are closed due to snow.

5. The UK is a wonderful place for young

people but many of our youths get a bad press. There is in fact only one small group of particularly troublesome young people, known as the Cabinet.

6. There's more to the United Kingdom than just London. If you've some time, have your driver take you around the country and meet some of the locals. One's been doing that for years and it's well worth a trip, one can assure you.

7. A key constitutional principle in the United Kingdom is a strong political opposition to the Government of the day. At the moment it is Labour, headed by Ed Miliband who you may recognise from his acting days as Mr Bean.

8. Train travel is a wonderful way of seeing all the UK has to offer. If you happen to have the entire GDP of Romania in your pocket, you can get as far as Watford if travelling off peak and cattle class.

9. Euros are not accepted. In any shape or form. Anywhere. Ever.

10. You may find it hard to adjust to living in a country that never wins the Eurovision Song Contest. Do try and remember that this is because Europeans have no taste and not because the British have no talent.

One hopes these few tips will make integrating into the UK a pleasant experience. If, however, you wish to remain put and still experience the benefits of Royal leadership, fear not: no matter where you are in the world, you can rest assured that the British will get to you eventually.

As ever your loving Queen.

7

From the
Royal Notebook

Words One Has Learned Since Prince George was Born

Having a baby heir in the Palace was like learning an entirely new language.

1. Dummy: one thought it a term of endearment for Ed Miliband.
2. Nappy: positive that was where Prince Edward goes after lunchy.
3. Breast pump: quite convinced that was one of Camilla's "me time" toys.
4. Bib: stands for Breakfast in Bed as far as one's concerned.
5. Crib: George Osborne's term for his official residence at 11 Downing Street.
6. Bottle: of gin? Is there another kind?
7. Rattle: the only rattle one has experienced is on the wheel of the Bentley.

8. Mobile: apparently hangs over a cot. Strange, one usually uses it for tweeting when one's out and about.

9. Bouncer: the Royal official who removes the PM after his weekly audience.

10. Steriliser: the gentleman we sent the DoE to after Prince Edward was born.

11. Formula: the only formula on one's mind is the one used to calculate the Civil List payments.

12. Play Pen: absolutely sure this is what Nick Clegg used before he had a real pen (temporarily actually – we had to swap it back after he kept drawing on the downstairs loo wall at Downing Street).

Royals for Hire

Thinking of inviting a member of one's family to open your hospital/bridge/parliament/country? The top five most requested Royals are:

One. Of course. After sixty years on the throne and on the gin, one is still the world's best-selling Royal. Queen of Queens.

The Duchess of Cornwall. A surprise at number two, but HRH the Duchess of Cornwall shot up the list when England retained the ashes and it was revealed that this year they were genuine ashes from Camilla's cigars.

Prince Harry. The world's most eligible bachelor. Clothes not included.

Princess Beatrice. The Grand Old Duke of York does not have 10,000 men; that is just his PR. He does, however, have two daughters. Princess Beatrice shot from minor royal to first class fashion disaster with her choice of hat for the Royal Wedding. Remarkably like a Pretzel in shape and colour, Princess Beatrice is now a top five selling royal.

The Duke of Edinburgh. Yes, bless him, the original playboy prince. Grandfather to the nation, royal enforcer in chief and a bloody good laugh, the DoE.

Narrowly missing out on the top five was Prince Charles. On hearing the news, he sent this text: "If someone would just move over and give me a chance I'd really appreciate it." Awkward.

Sandringham Etiquette

Christmas is that time of the year when we come together as friends and families to celebrate the year past and look forward to the year ahead. Yet your Queen knows better than anyone that such times can be as stressful as they are happy.

Whilst chaos reigns on the continent, thankfully we British are blessed with a high level of etiquette to keep everything in shape. Here are one's top Christmas etiquette rules, as observed at Sandringham.

1. You may be tempted to invest in a large Christmas tree to encourage feelings of envy amongst your friends and neighbours but always remember that a tree more than 100ft tall is just showing off. And under no

circumstances should the tree touch the ceiling of your ballroom.

2. Tinsel is never acceptable as a decoration on this side of the Channel. And it is certainly never acceptable to make a dress out of it, Edward.

3. It is never appropriate to have in-laws over for Christmas lunch. Ever. No matter how much they insist that they are part of the (Royal) family. Is that clear, Mr and Mrs Middleton?

4. If, like one, you have a grandson who likes to spend Christmas in the nude, politely remind him that he is not in Vegas now and that no one wants to see the crown jewels whilst tucking into a goose.

5. Goose. Not turkey. Not an Asda "Three Bird Roast for under a fiver". Goose.

6. Always buy a bigger goose than you imagine necessary. There should always be enough to go around. If there's one rule Prince Andrew lives by it is to make sure you stuff an extra large bird at Christmas.

7. If your son is next in line to the throne, it is considered the height of rudeness to comment that a Christmas party hat is the closest he'll get to a crown for a while.

8. Watching one's speech at 3pm on Christmas Day is absolutely non-negotiable. Watching it on a phone, on "catch up" or on ITV is actually a criminal offence and, be assured, one will prosecute.

9. If, like one, you invite family and friends over for a fancy dress party on Christmas evening, always be extra clear on your instructions.

10. Following a Christmas Day full of food and drink, a light breakfast is the order of the morning on Boxing Day. Try black pudding, baked beans, fried eggs, sausages, fried potatoes, mushrooms and tomatoes to cleanse the system.

Wanted: Housekeeper
Fit for a Queen

Queen of sixteen sovereign nations, head of the commonwealth, defender of the faith and supreme governor of the Church of England seeks an experienced housekeeper/spy/cocktail-maker to look after a small 1,000 year old castle in Berkshire. Benefits include a modest six bedroom apartment and a share of various hereditary estate incomes. To apply, text anyone you like and GCHQ will call you straight back.

Department
Master of the Household's Office, DoE's directorate.

Location
Windsor Castle.

Wanted: Housekeeper Fit for a Queen

Starting Salary
£35,000 per annum plus a percentage of the rent from approximately two thirds of Cornwall.

Hours of work
20 hours per day (gin breaks are provided).

Contract Type
Meaningless, one is the Queen.

Accommodation available?
Small six bedroom three floor apartment with views over the Great Park.

Mandatory Requirements
An experienced Housekeeper with an in-depth understanding of the highest standards of services and practices in cocktail making. A distinct dislike of politicians would be an advantage.

Job Description
The sun never sets on the British Empire.

Thankfully it does set on Windsor Castle and when it does, Her Majesty the Queen requires a well-made bed with a gin cocktail beside it. That, in a nutshell, is your job.

As Head Housekeeper you will oversee the Housekeeping teams at Windsor Castle and Frogmore House, ensuring that all 700 rooms are vacuumed at least once a day, or immediately after visiting politicians or Middletons have left the room, whichever is more frequent.

You will be required to remember detailed instructions for making up visitors' rooms, such as placing a number of frozen peas under the mattress of politicians, dipping a cigar in gin and leaving it next to the bed of the Duchess of Cornwall, ensuring that there is no one with a camera phone in Prince Harry's room, and plugging in the thing that projects stars on the ceiling if Mr Clegg is staying (he has awful trouble getting off to sleep without it).

Wanted: Housekeeper Fit for a Queen

Person Specification

- A deep, in-built hatred of politicians is a distinct advantage
- Discretion is absolutely key. You must keep whatever you hear in visitors' rooms absolutely confidential until you report it verbatim to Her Majesty the Queen
- The ability to make a decent gin cocktail without siphoning off the Royal Gin for yourself
- A bit handy with a hoover

Draft Queen's Speech for the State Opening of Parliament

State Opening of Parliament tomorrow. No doubt the sunshine won't last. The DoE says that getting a horse-drawn carriage out is practically akin to doing a rain dance. Still, it's nice to take the crown out for a spin.

Wallace and Gromit (Cameron and Clegg) have sent over a draft of one's speech for one to read out, but this year one has decided to surprise them with a little speech of one's own...

My Lords and Members of the House of Commons,

My government's legislative programme will focus on appearing to make progress whilst in reality being deadlocked by infighting, incompetence and sheer lack of creativity or common sense, thus continuing a political tradition that dates back for at least one hundred years.

My ministers' first priority will be to find ways of leveraging more and more money from the depths of our pockets to spend on spurious and self-indulgent schemes that, at best, do absolutely nothing for My people and in all likelihood piss us all off or make life more difficult than it is already.

Legislation will be introduced to create an illusion of activity and to keep one's ever expanding political establishment occupied.

For these reasons, one has decided to dissolve parliament once and for all and adopt a system of Government that makes altogether a great deal more sense: absolute monarchy.

The immediate and complete abandonment of almost all Government departments and

the salary and expense savings of former MPs,
peers and those who support them will clear
the United Kingdom's budget deficit and debt in
approximately three weeks.

Taxes for all subjects will be drastically reduced
and calculated in future in accordance with the
following formula: we shall tax the minimum
required to do what we need; we will spend only
what we have and additional taxes will be raised
for overseas educational projects (wars).

Independence of the United States of America will be
revoked. They have had long enough to prove they
can govern themselves and others without Royal
guidance and quite frankly enough is enough.

Legislation will be introduced requiring
horsemeat to be labelled as such.

Legislation will be introduced making every
Monday a Bank Holiday and requiring
compulsory closure at midday on a Friday.

Draft Queen's Speech

Working weekends will not be permitted (unless selling gin or running a betting shop).

Newspapers will not be allowed to print anything that they cannot indisputably prove is completely true. They will also not be allowed to publish the Duchess of Cambridge's breasts or Prince Harry's crown jewels. This will not require editors to meet for lunch to oversee the system.

All TV celebrities circa 1967 to 1989 will be rounded up and imprisoned, just in case.

The United Kingdom will withdraw from the European Union and the Eurovision Song Contest and the RAF will be popping over to collect every penny one has ever paid. Plus interest. At 700% APR. Plus fees.

France will officially be merged with the Isle of Wight.

With immediate effect it shall be illegal to be Jessie

*J, Justin Bieber or One Direction in a public place.
It will also be illegal for Paul McCartney or Elton
John to perform at official public events, or any
event attended by a member of the Royal Family.*

*The Prince of Wales will attend the
Commonwealth Heads of Government meeting in
Sri Lanka and deliver this speech to the assembled
nations.*

*Prince Philip and I look forward to Royal Ascot
this summer, where one's success or otherwise on
the horses will dictate in large part the amount of
tax that one shall be collecting over the next year.*

Other measures will be laid before you.

*My Lords and members of the House of
Commons, I pray that the blessing of almighty
God may rest upon your counsels.*

William and Catherine Congratulations Card Messages

Had some lovely messages from assembled heads of Government and State in a little card they'd sent around to mark Prince George's birth:

- Congratulations William and Catherine and Pharaoh Elizabeth from all the people and the first elected Government of Egy… (unfinished, must have been interrupted)
- U can share my sandpit xox Love from Nicky Clegg xox
- Congratulations! Sorry we couldn't afford to send a present – had to save up for a stamp! Love from the Queen of Spain x
- Hope you've paid your health insurance! Just kidding! Congratulations, love the Obamas xx

- Tell me I'm not paying for the Christening?! Angela Merkel
- Only sixty years until the little one can abdicate! Trust me, it's all the rage! Love from the ex-King of the Belgians ;-)
- Love from Edward Snowden! Joke! Congratulations from President Putin
- All very best wishes from everyone down under! Love Kevin Rudd/Julia Gillard (delete as appropriate!) xx
- Is this some kind of joke?! I will make an official complaint to the UN about this card. President of Argentina
- A new monarch for an independent Scotland! ASx
- Wonderful news! Will be celebrating by releasing the dismal economic figures whilst no one is looking! Dave x
- All best wishes (sorry we couldn't send a present – Angela Merkel said no!) love from all in Greece xx
- Life on the outside is gooooooooood! Love ex-Queen of the Netherlands (Now FREE!) xxxxx

- Yay! I'm not the youngest ruler anymore! Kim Jong Un
- Je refuse d'écrire en anglais. M Hollande
- We're having a street carnival in celebration! (Honest, it's just a street carnival) Love from Brazil x
- Come and live here. We will never let anyone have you. From Ecuador

The Royal iPod

Top ten songs on the Royal iPod:

1. 'God Save the Queen' NOT the Sex Pistols version
2. 'I Want to Break Free' (Nigel Farage's European Anthem)
3. 'Wind Beneath my Wings' (Mr Clegg and Mr Cameron's "special" song)
4. 'We Will Rock You' (played during visits by the French as a warning)
5. 'Handbags and Gladrags' (Mrs Thatcher's favourite)
6. 'All I need is a Miracle' (Ed Miliband's election song)
7. 'Here You Come Again' (Prince Andrew and the Duchess of York's song)
8. 'Don't Stop Believing' (The Archbishop of Canterbury's favourite)

9. 'Diamonds and Pearls' (played during the State Opening of Parliament)
10. 'God Save the Queen Live' (played by Brian May from the roof of Buckingham Palace every morning as one's personal wake up call)

The Best of Britain

One's soft power is legendary in international circles, of course. Whilst the Americans and the Chinese posture, one is quietly getting on with the business of world stewardship. One used to call it empire, these days one likes to think of it more as maternal guidance.

Ten things that make Britain the greatest nation on earth:

1. **The English language**: English has become the international language of choice, but let's not forget that it was invented here and has become our most successful export. All those years of sailing around the world teaching the locals to speak properly is our greatest gift to the world.

2. **Music**: The country that gave the world Queen, the Beatles and Led Zeppelin. British music is the soundtrack to lives the world over. Yes, it's gone downhill a bit recently with One Direction, but no country rocks like the British.

3. **Humour**: The British sense of humour is legendary, as demonstrated by our choice of Deputy Prime Minister. Unlike the Germans, who have absolutely no conception of humour whatsoever, the British have a finely tuned ability to laugh at ourselves and, most importantly, at other nations.

4. **The Olympics**: Nobody does it better. It's little wonder they keep coming back for more. London has hosted the Olympic Games more often than any other city. The greatest show on earth in the greatest city on earth, it's only right.

5 **Democracy**: There is nothing more satisfying than seeing a Government kicked out on its arse – a gift given to

millions around the globe by the British. Democracy was invented in Britain and no one lectures the world about it better than the British.

6. **Bacon and egg sandwiches**: Pretention may be the name of the game in French cooking, but no one does hangover cures better than the British. The DoE's bacon and egg sandwiches are known the world over and have been a highlight for visiting heads of state for six decades.

7. **The stiff upper lip**: Whilst other nations flail around like sea lions at times of national crisis, the British remain calm, resolute and composed. Even in the face of unthinkable pain, such as Girls Aloud reforming, we keep calm and carry on.

8. **Gin**: oiling the wheels of state since 1952.

9. **James Bond**: The epitome of Britain. Strong, sophisticated, understated, witty, adaptable, stylish.

10. **The Queen**: A global icon, a figure of stability in a changing world, charm

personified. Queen of sixteen sovereign nations, head of the commonwealth, supreme governor of the Church of England, defender of the faith. Your Queen loves you.

Acknowledgements
To The Royal Household

One should like to thank one's hundreds of thousands of Twitter followers, past and present. You have been with your Queen for many years and your support and incessant retweeting is a great comfort to one. You are all Knights and Ladies of the Order of the Tweet and as such you are accorded the style and privileges this rank brings (namely not having to go to work on a Tuesday – if anyone asks, tell them the Queen said it was OK).

One's heartfelt thanks and appreciation to one's Literary Division, in particular The Lady Sarah Williams and all at Ed Victor Literary Agents, to one's editor Colonel Andrew Lockett (who is more than a throat sweet in one's eyes) and all at Duckworth Publishers, and to one's commercial agent – whose name is a state secret. Your dedication in the name of One's Majesty is a joy to behold.

Most of all, thank you to one's Imperial Family, who through thick and thin are a source of such support, love and happiness that one really would not know where one would be without them. And one's two Princesses especially, who are the brightest stars in one's sky.

And of course Her Majesty Queen Elizabeth II, who through one's entire lifetime has been a beacon of dedication and grace. God bless you ma'am.